CHAMBERSBURG, FRONTIER TOWN, 1730-1794

A BICENTENNIAL NARRATIVE
OF THE ORIGIN AND GROWTH OF
CHAMBERSBURG
AND FRANKLIN COUNTY IN PENNSYLVANIA

By

Paul Swain Havens
President Emeritus, Wilson College

Copyright © 1975, Paul Swain Havens

Printed in the USA by:

The Craft Press, Inc.
Chambersburg, Pa.

CHAMBERS FORT

Artists rendering by M. H. Gemmill

TO
THE EARLY SETTLERS
WHOSE UNCONQUERABLE WILL
TAMED THE FRONTIER LANDS
OF PENNSYLVANIA

They builded better than they knew

CONTENTS

ABBREVIATIONS

c: circa; about, near
D.A.B.: *Dictionary of American Biography*
D.N.B.: *Dictionary of National Biography* (British)
ed.: editor, edited by
Enc. Brit.: *Encyclopedia Britannica*
ff.: and the following
ibid.: the same volume, article, work
i.e.: id est; that is
KHSP: Kittochtinny Historical Society Papers
MS: manuscript
n.d.: no date
n. pub: no publisher given
op. cit.: the volume previously quoted
Pa. Arch.: *Pennsylvania Archives*
passim: everywhere, throughout
vv.: volumes

FOREWORD

This narrative will excite little interest among those who are well acquainted with the history of Chambersburg, of Franklin County, and of the Cumberland Valley. It contains little that is new. It cannot properly be called a research work, but only an assembling of many facts, opinions, and judgments already known and stated. Its purpose, then, is not to present hitherto unknown data, but only to weave an account of events and people in Chambersburg and the surrounding community in a generally chronological order, placing these events and these people in the broader context of the events in the state and the nation that affected the Valley. It is a work for the person who wishes to know something about the origins and history of Chambersburg and its environs but has not had the time or incentive to investigate them.

The original suggestion was that a written Bicentennial account should be prepared about Chambersburg in the years from 1770 to 1790. This has proved impossible for two reasons. The events of this span of twenty years are significant only in the context of what happened before and what happened after. Again, Chambersburg cannot be isolated out by an historical scalpel, so to speak, from its surrounding community. In the earliest years there was no Chambersburg, only the Conococheague Settlement, only the Cumberland Valley. All the early settlers knew one another personally, experienced the same problems and dangers and pleasures, and were a scattered but real geographical unit. While this narrative focuses on Chambersburg and Franklin County, it moves outside whenever I believe it will benefit by a broader perspective.

The boundaries of this narrative are loosely the years 1730 and 1794, the year of Benjamin Chambers's arrival in the Great Valley and the year of the conclusion of the Whiskey Rebellion. At a few points the story reaches earlier and later, but in general these are the principal years of the tale.

This span of two generations saw more changes in the Cumberland Valley, and more rapid changes, than any comparable period in our history. From uninhabited forest and hunting land, the lower Cumberland Valley evolved gradually into a well populated, well cultivated, and prosperous region. Its growth from empty land to a cohesive community of hard-working and self-respecting people is one of the great achievements of the American frontier of the eighteenth century. It is this story that is the subject of this volume.

The qualities which above all else marked these first settlers—Scotch-Irish and Germans alike—were energy and endurance. The crude physical energy required to tame the forest land and make it yield a living was immense. But the energy was there. We are told that the founder of the town of Scotland, Alexander Thompson, with the help of three sons cleared 50 acres of land in the first year of his arrival, 1771-72.[1] This may be an exaggeration—for this achievement sounds almost impossible—but it suggests that these people could and did perform vast feats of sheer muscular strength. They knew nothing of the eight-hour day. They worked from sunrise to sunset. Their very lives depended on their energy, and they met the challenge and survived.

As for endurance, the account of it is writ large in the resistance they offered to the Indian attacks that killed their families, kidnapped their children, burned their homes and barns, and scorched their crops. It is true that many fled. Who can blame them? Yet it is equally true that the Indians' cruelties never conquered them, never drove them totally away, never broke their spirit. In spite of all the terror, the hardship, and the uncertainty of their future, these people endured and remained. If they had not possessed these attributes of energy and endurance, this treatise would never have been written.

In the extant accounts on which we have to depend for information about these early years, we miss certain things. Let us list a few.

We miss humor. These settlers were serious-minded and religious. They must have laughed, but there is no echo of hearty laughter anywhere in the printed record of these times. Now and again the reader will smile, but it is hard to find any evidence of spontaneous humor.

We miss conversation. Their daily life must have been full of it, as ours is, but no one had the time—or took the trouble—to record what they said to one another. If we had only a few records of daily conversation, our knowledge of these people would be greatly enhanced.

In the same vein, we miss romance. We know of mills, forts and cannons, land-deeds and military preparations, but we hear little about the proposals of marriage that obviously took place or about the brides and bridegrooms of the time. All we know is wedding dates—and few enough of these. No record tells explicitly of a courtship; no record includes a word of endearment.

And we miss evidence of fun and play. Surely there must have been amusements, even among the strict Presbyterians, German Reformed, Lutherans, and Mennonites. A community cannot exist without some fun and games; but on this topic there is almost complete silence.

We must name one other thing we miss: a newspaper or any other such avenue of communication with the outer world. What news came from Philadelphia, Baltimore, or Boston was weeks late and usually inaccurate, warped by passage from mouth to mouth over many inhospitable miles. Benjamin Franklin's *Pennsylvania Gazette* was founded in 1729, but its news was largely confined to the seaboard. The first newspaper in Chambersburg came in 1790.

These frontier people were warm, energetic, able, and very normal human beings, with all the attributes of character, both domestic and communal, that we expect of those who have chosen the frontier way of life. Yet the remaining documents do not tell us all we wish to know. For this reason I have included among the Appendices a few "Imaginary Incidents" (each prefaced as such) that have no documentation whatsoever. No historical account contains them; they are pure fiction. I include them because the historical record is almost wholly devoid of the kind of humble, human stories that give life to what otherwise is a mere skeleton. Their sources are the impressions I have formed of people, of incidents, of the climate of opinion of the time, of the probabilities as I saw them, and of the psychology of those whom I met in my reading. I cannot say that these things happened. I can only say that something like them might have happened. Not history, certainly, but I hope not wholly out of order. Writing them has been a welcome foil to what I have elsewhere attempted to present with historical accuracy.

We must now say a word about the Kittochtinny Historical Society, founded in 1898 by Dr. S. A. Martin, then President of Wilson College. The fifteen volumes of printed papers of the Society contain a vast amount of historical information about this community, ranging from the early days to the contemporary scene. These volumes embrace about 150 or more papers, each carefully prepared for reading at a meeting of the Society and for publication later. They are a mine of facts for anyone interested in the history of the region; indeed, they are one of the best reservoirs of historical information in the Cumberland Valley.

The authors of these studies were—and are—for the most part amateur historians. As we read these papers, we find contradictions and obvious inaccuracies. This is inevitable. There are also some proof-reading errors, especially with respect to dates. Some of our local compositors must have had little sense of history and, without thinking, produced 1864 when the proper date was 1764. There are several instances of this carelessness. Nevertheless, these papers are among our most precious historical doucments. To them I am deeply indebted for facts not elsewhere available. I have leaned heavily upon them not only because they offer valuable information but also because I believe the Society should be recognized for its achievements and encouraged to continue its work of discovering facts of Cumberland Valley history.

The writing of this volume is the first occasion, I believe, when the findings of the Society have been assimilated into a consecutive historical narrative. It is fitting that a Bicentennial study of Chambersburg and Franklin County should incorporate the work of so many men and women who have cherished their own history and illuminated it through their research. Indeed, a large part of this narrative may be said to have been written by members of the Society, as study of the footnotes will show. The present author's role has been to arrange these findings and present them in a new context.

I wish to acknowledge with gratitude the always courteous and efficient services of members of the staff of the Coyle Free Library of Chambersburg; the patience of Mrs. Lucy Chambers Benchoff, Mr. James Walker and my son, Professor T. R. H. Havens, in reading the manuscript and their many useful suggestions; the industry and accuracy of Miss Doris Whiteman in typing the manuscript; and the support and interest at all times of members of the Chambersburg Bicentennial Committee, of which Mayor J. William Stover is Chairman.

P.S.H.

PROLOGUE

Many writers have told us that four Chambers brothers, James, Robert, Joseph and Benjamin, came to America about 1725 from Ulster and settled on land near Fishing Creek, on the Susquehanna River about ten miles north of the present city of Harrisburg. Here they built a grist mill. A few years later, about 1730, they crossed the river into the Great Valley (later to be called the Cumberland Valley). James settled at the Big Spring, Robert at the Middle Spring, and Benjamin and Joseph at the confluence of the Falling Spring and the Conococheague. Benjamin built a house and a grist mill; and from this modest beginning came Chambersburg. Joseph returned to Fishing Creek to oversee the property there.

But this is indeed a threadbare account. Who were the Chambers brothers? Where did they come from? What brought them to this country? Why did so many Scotch-Irish folk come after them, wave on wave? Why did Germans also come in equal or greater numbers, sharing the lands of the Valley and bringing with them another culture?

Most of the English Colonies in America were founded by people of pure Anglo-Saxon stock, and each colony had usually a religion of its own, with comparatively little intermixture of other faiths. Virginia and the New England colonies were particularly pure in their people and religion, and the history of each of them is the simple story of a people of one language, nation, and religion, thoroughly homogeneous, and always acting as a unit. But Pennsylvania was altogether different, and no other

colony had such a mixture of languages, nationalities, and religions. Dutch, Swedes, English,
Germans, Scotch-Irish, Welsh; Quakers, Presbyterians, Episcopalians, Lutherans, Reformed, Mennonites, Tunkers, and Moravians, all had a share in
creating it.[1]

Of these many strains we shall have to do with two:
the Scotch-Irish and the Germans; and in order to understand why they left their native countries and came to a
distant and virtually unknown province, we must go back
some years in history. Only thus can we understand the
motives of these people and the pressures that led them
into their bold adventure.

The Scotch-Irish

The term is a misnomer though it is widely used.
The proper term is "Scots in Ireland".

But how did it come about that thousands of Scots
lived for a century or more in Ireland and emigrated—
many of them—from Ireland to America?

For many centuries Ireland had been a thorn in
English flesh. Inhabited by a people of a different race,
different religion, and different customs, Ireland seemed
to the English a land of wild, savage, and uncultured
kerns. Yet the two islands were separated at one point by
only twenty miles of sea. The enemies of England have
always seen Ireland as a possible staging ground for an
attack on England. Philip of Spain, for example,
designed his Armada of 1596-1597 and his invasion fleet
of 1599 to open up an Irish front.[2] His plan failed, as did
a similar project of the Germans in the First World War.
Yet the danger remained.

Moreover, the Irish were uncivilized not only in

English eyes but also in European eyes generally. The Spanish detested them; but to the English they represented a cultural menace too close geographically to be lightly tolerated.

Since the time of the Statutes of Kilkenny under Edward III, a system of legislative *apartheid* had been imposed to keep the English and Anglo-Irish of the Pale from being infected by the barbarous customs of the natives. They might not sell horses to the Irish, or armour or weapons, or consort with them, or intermarry, or wear Irish dress.[3]

Queen Elizabeth undertook to deal with the Irish problem by encouraging English settlers to open up large 'plantations'. Perhaps English influence and example would civilize the Irish. Her plan failed. By 1592, "of 58 'plantations' undertaken, only 13 remained, and no more than 245 English families had actually settled on the land."[4] Life among the Irish was too dangerous: plundering, burning, waylaying, and no protection anywhere.

Her successor, James I, inherited the Irish problem when he ascended the throne in 1603, and he sought to solve it in much the same way. He was himself a Scotsman and a staunch Protestant and believed that his fellow-Scots might succeed where the earlier English settlers had failed. Under his encouragement many Scots emigrated to northern Ireland, where the land was fertile and the climate milder than their own.

The connection with English-ruled Ireland after 1603 made possible an enduring change there in the early seventeenth century, the colonization of Ulster after 1606 with lowland Scots. Ulster had been the most recalcitrant province of Ireland under

Elizabeth: as a result there were forfeitures to exploit and frequent war had reduced the population. Scots went in and settled, sometimes on their own initiative, more often in organized groups whose leaders competed for grants from the forfeitûres. This sort of colonization did not call for large amounts of capital: supplies could be sent in driblets across the narrow gap of the Irish channel as required. Kin would gradually follow a leader across. Slowly through the first half of the century the Scottish settlement grew: probably by mid-century the Scots in Ireland numbered 50,000, perhaps more. This again was a threat to Gaelic society, separating its two sections. It made it certain that events in Ireland would be closely felt in Scotland.[5]

These Scots in Ireland were a hardy folk. They lived much to themselves: they were clannish in the literal sense. They regarded the Irish in the southern counties very much as some of their descendants were later to regard the American Indians, *i.e.*, as semi-savages, uncivilized and unfriendly. Even at this late date in history there was almost no inter-marriage, not only because of cultural differences but also because the Irish were Roman Catholics and the Scots almost without exception Presbyterians.

All went well during the reign of James I. The newcomers made Ulster flourish. But under Charles I (1625-49) persecutions of a sort began. Charles wished to enforce the use of the Anglican Prayer Book; but to the sensitive nostrils of the Presbyterians the Prayer Book smelt of popery. Moreover, the Scots were stiff-necked and not to be forced into anything against their will. In 1640 the Roman Catholics rose against the Protestants

16

and killed many of them. And then their own King, now Charles II (1660-85), decreed tolerance for Roman Catholics and laid sharp restrictions on the freedom of worship of the Presbyterians and Independents. Even worse was the brief reign of James II (1685-88). Protestants were openly persecuted, their industries dissolved, their holdings seized, their lives and livelihood in constant danger. This was the time when the notorious Claverhouse was persecuting their kin in Scotland, especially the Covenanters. They were hard years for Protestants on both sides of the water.

The Covenanters represented the quintessence of Protestantism in an already Protestant country. So strong was the anti-Catholic feeling during the reign of James II that, whether they' wished to or not, most Protestants subscribed to the Covenant:

> "We promise, and sweare by the Great Name of the Lord our God, to continue in the Profession and Obedience of the Foresaid Religion: That we shall defend the same and resist all these contrary errours and corruptions, according to our vocation, and to the uttermost of that power that God hath put in our hands, all the dayes of our life."

The meaning of the Covenant that so many of the Scots had subscribed is worth a little attention. On the one hand it was a generalized form of the old rebellious Band which Scottish nobles were accustomed to form when they planned a stroke for power. But the religious overtones of the word soon overshadowed this aspect: it was not only a Band between men but an undertaking to God. By keeping it the Scots would emulate the Jews as a chosen people. A generation of men and women reared on biblical story, in which God had safeguarded and preserved his people against enormous odds, could easily grow to see the Covenant as a means by which something special lay in store for them. From this came two of the characteristics of the later Covenanters, a narrow national conceit and a belief that the normal needs of support for a movement— political backing and military strength—could be ignored. God would secure the victory of his own in his own cause against all odds; the cause would be made known by those who claimed to have direct authority and guidance; the generals and the politicians must do what ministers and mystics decreed.[6]

The Covenanters' stiffnecked opposition to any form of religion or government that did not match their beliefs as set forth in the Covenant, supported by their mystical belief in themselves as a new chosen people, sealed their minds to any kind of accommodation or compromise and invited persecution by their enemies.

Not even the Protestant William of Orange (William III), who came to the throne in 1689, could stem the evil tide of persecution. The Scottish Presbyterians who had defended Enniskillen and Londonderry against James II and his Cathloic troops "were treated little better than the Catholics who besieged them."[7] Protestants by the hundreds were turned off their lands by absentee landlords. Many were in poverty and turned to violence.

Broken keep and burning farm
Taught his fathers strength of arm.
Feud and fight from gate to gate
Showed them how to nurse their hate.[8]

18

The division of the Gaelic or Scottish community into two parts, the larger in Scotland and the more energetic and adventuresome in Ireland, proved to be important historically to both segments in their relations with America. Kinship was a very powerful force among the Scots; and the little passage of water between Scotland and northern Ireland did not diminish it. When a Scottish family living in Ulster migrated to America, there was created a strong magnet to draw kinfolk in Scotland to follow. What was a promising adventure for the relatives in Ireland would probably be a good thing also for the Scottish branch of the family.

The Scots in Scotland were given another impulse westward by the failure of the Stuart cause in 1715 and 1746. Many of them, strongly supporting the Stuart claim to the throne of Britain, were left outcasts—men without a future at home— when that claim finally foundered at Culloden. Their fathers and grandfathers might have been content to seek refuge across the channel in Ireland. But Ireland was not a happy haven in those years, and so they embarked for the New World and became, not the Scots in Ireland, but the Scots in America, straight from the southern Highlands and the Border Country around Ayrshire, Kirkcudbrightshire, and Wigtownshire. Some of them were professional soldiers and found their training useful in the troubled times of 1755-64. Covenanters and mere orthodox Presbyterians alike brought their religious convictions with them, but in the new land the differences, while quite visible at first, were gradually eroded by the common demands of frontier life. And within a generation or two, by a gentle and ironic twist of history, the Scots of Scotland and the Scots of Ireland became in the public mind one folk known only, then and now, as Scotch-Irish.

These, then, are some of the conditions that caused the beginning of the migration westward. The Scots of Ireland by 1700 were the grandchildren of these who had migrated from Scotland under James I and his successors. Many of them had grown up on stories of the Border Country between England and Scotland and of the battles fought there. And now they too had lived in a kind of border country where they had had to fight to live. Many, of course, had died: it was the survival of the fittest; and it was these hardy survivors and their descendants who came to America. It was mostly the young men and their families who came, and in many instances they had encouragement from enterprising land agents at home and across the Atlantic.

> For centuries it had been the custom that the second and younger sons follow the life of adventure of the soldier or sailor and whenever it could be arranged—perhaps by the mother—a younger son studied for the ministry and the preaching of the Gospel.

> Many of these young men did not want to cast their lots with the mother country and became susceptible to the advertisements of the new land across the water. Indeed there were advertisements, and many of them, all describing this land of America as a spearhead of adventure. One most famous account is labeled, *History of Pensilvania*, published in London in 1698 by Gabriel Thomas. This was reprinted by A. Monroe Aurand, Jr., in 1935. The language is flowery enough to persuade even the author to wish that "Pensilvania" were the land of milk and honey mentioned by Mr. Thomas.[9]

When did the migration begin? Where did the immigrants go? The first settlement of Sctoch-Irish in America occurred as early as 1632 along the Eastern Shore of Maryland when this new land was granted to Lord Baltimore;[10] but the migration began in earnest about 1718 or 1719 after a series of bad harvests in Ulster. The immigrants landed at Philadelphia after a sea-journey of two months or more during which they endured many hardships. From Philadelphia they went north to Bucks County or south to Chester County; and a few, like the Chambers brothers, pushed their way along the Susquehanna. This great river remained a barrier to further migration for some years for reasons we shall see later. But finally the four Chambers brothers burst across the barrier about 1730, making their way down what was later to be called the Cumberland Valley.

The Pennsylvania Germans

We must now ask much the same questions about the Pennsylvania Germans as we have asked about the Scotch-Irish. Who were they? Where did they come from? Why did they migrate to America?

We might begin by citing a comparison between the Scotch-Irish and the Germans.

All fingers in Ulster, in the young Eighteenth century, pointed to the New World, and men, women and children, were not wanting to obey the summons. They began to come to Pennsylvania about 1719, and soon formed the most numerous and influential element in the colony. The Germans, to whom far greater inducements had been offered to settle in Pennsylvania, were after all aliens, special oaths were administered to them of allegiance to

21

the British Crown, and they remained quite as German after they came as they were before, and until this day the Pennsylvania Germans are a class of their own. Other nationalities have come here, perhaps retaining some distinctive appellation, though little more, to show whence they came. But the Pennsylvania Germans to-day are as unbroken a body as when they first stepped off their ships, with a language, with manners and customs still all and only their own. These peculiarities have kept them in the background as a factor in the political life of the nation, and while they have always been distinguished for their essential qualities of morality, bravery, loyalty and all the other qualities of good private citizens, they have by no means played that part in the formation of the typical American character to which their numbers and wealth entitle them, while their more turbulent and adventurous fellow colonists, the Scotch, who by 1770 formed one-third the population of Pennsylvania, on the contrary have been one of the most potent factors in the development of the country. They were indeed the first expansionists.[11]

These comments, though suggestive and helpful, need to be refined. We have found that the term Scotch-Irish is imprecise; so also is the term Pennsylvania German. For the Pennsylvania Germans were not all Germans. Many were German-speaking Swiss; others were Dutch. It is true that they all spoke the German language, a fact that was both a strength and a handicap when they came to America.

We must distinguish between two quite different waves of German immigration. The first was prompted by William Penn himself, who had travelled extensively in Germany and Holland and had met and admired the followers of Menno Simons (1492-1559). Like the Quakers, the Mennonites abhorred war, objected to oaths, to paid clergy, and to infant baptism. Many of them were pietists, seekers after the "Inner Light".

Thus when Penn received his vast grand of land in America from Charles II in 1681, he encouraged his Mennonite acquaintances to come to Penn's Woods. They responded instantly. A large colony established itself about eleven miles north of the site of Philadelphia and assumed the name of Germantown. Its leader was a man of remarkable ability and unquestioned piety, Francis Daniel Pastorius. Like the Quakers again, these Mennonites believed fervidly in religious toleration and so welcomed to their community Tunkers (Dunkards) and other sects who fled from persecution at home. Some of the Tunkers became the German Seventh-Day Baptists and founded a cloister at Ephrata peopled by celibate mystics known for their elaborate hymn-books and their love of music.

The community at Germantown had the dual amenities of wealth and culture. A school was founded in the early years; one of the first printing-presses in America was established; and Christopher Saur, a man of great influence among his compatriots, printed one of the first newspapers in the colony and manufactured in 1738 the first font of type made in America. The new town was incorporated in 1691; and "for fully a century Germantown was the headquarters of the Pennsylvania Dutch and the German-Americans".[12]

There was little German immigration during the next twenty years, but from 1702 onward increasing numbers came. This second wave was totally different from the first in many respects. It was vastly larger, vastly poorer, and much less civilized. It consisted mostly of peasants of Lutheran or Reformed background from the Palatinate, many of whom were illiterate.

Even among those who were fleeing from cruel persecution, and deserved the sympathy and assistance of every enlightened man, there appear to have been large numbers whose appearance was not at all unlikely to arouse prejudice among English colonists. They had come from mountain fastnesses or from obscure country districts, where they had been hiding; they had suffered hardships in reaching the sea, and still greater hardships on the two months' voyage. Their dress was peculiar; many of them were staring and strange like wild animals, carried weapons, and spoke an unintelligible dialect; they wore huge wooden shoes; and the men who settled in Lancaster were described as wearing long red caps and the women without either hats or caps, tying a string over their heads to keep the hair from their faces . . .

The reason for the change of character in the German immigrants after 1702 seems to have been the adoption of a new policy by Queen Anne, who ascended the throne in that year. Anne and her ministry seem to have been impressed with the idea that it would strengthen the British Empire to keep the English more at home on their island and fill up the colonies with Germans, or any unfortunate and cheap people from the Continent, provided they were Protestants and hostile to France and Spain.

To this end efforts were made to collect all the

discontented Germans, oppressed by war, poverty, persecution, and a disunited and broken country, and transport them to the colonies. In this attempt the Quakers as a sect do not seem to have taken much part. Their attention was confined chiefly to encouraging the peace sects who were in sympathy with themselves, and they cared nothing about the Lutherans and Reformed or the masses of the rough German peasantry.

The British government circulated books and papers in the Palatinate and other provinces to encourage emigration. The books had a picture of the queen, and a title-page in gold letters, and were long known among the poor people whom they were intended to influence as the Golden Books. They produced a great effect, and there was soon what has been called a landslide of humanity in the German population. During the two years 1708 and 1709 over thirty thousand of them crossed over to England.

The Golden Books and the devastation of war and persecution had been assisted by a very severe winter, in which birds and animals were frozen in the fields and men fell dead on the roads. For a time the government had more success with its new plan than it desired, for these people were utterly destitute, and created no little alarm and considerable riot among the lower classes. They were sheltered in tents on the commons and fields near London, and the process of transporting them to Pennsylvania, New York, and the Carolinas was begun . . . .

For many years large numbers continued to go to England to be shipped. But as time went on it became more and more the habit to transport them direct from their own country. The vessels that carried them from Germany usually touched at an English port to be cleared and have their cargo justified under the authority of the British government. A regular emigrant trade sprang up, and vessels were chartered to proceed to Rotterdam and load Palatines for Pennsylvania just as they were chartered for cargoes of rum, molasses, or negroes. The owners and captains were not altogether unlike the typical slavers, and the Palatine voyage to America was not far removed from the horrors of the middle passage.[13]

In one year alone nearly 12,000 of these immigrants arrived, Governor Keith in 1717 was uneasy because of the size of this invasion, fearing either that the Germans would turn Pennsylvania into a German province or that at the least they would become an indigestible state within a state. A few years later the Reverend Michael Schlatter, leader of the Reformed immigrants, and the Reverend Heinrich Melchior Muhlenberg, leader of the Lutherans, recognized these dangers—especially the second—and urged the Germans to learn English. Many, of course, opposed this advice, as some do even now.

Many of these poor peasants came to America as 'redemptioners'; i.e., since they had no money to pay their passage, they signed papers that made them practical serfs for a period of years, usually about seven, on their arrival. They hired themselves for whatever tasks their masters wished to impose upon them until the cost of the passage was 'redeemed'. This practice was widely abused and the redemptioners cruelly exploited. On the other hand, they represented a ready supply of unskilled labor

lear the forests, remove stumps, build cabins, plow
ds, plant crops and harvest them. Many ran away
fore they had paid off their debt of work, and the
iffs were busy finding them and returning them to
masters or putting them in debtor's prison. This is
of the more savory chapters of immigrant history.
other unsavory incident may be laid to the cu-
and treachery of Governor Hunter of New York.
luced a colony of Germans from the Palatinate to
and settle and then exploited and robbed them un-
onably. Hearing that conditions were better in
Woods and that the authorities were honest and
dly, they left for Pennsylvania, threading their way
in 1723 from New York down the Susquehanna to Tulpe-
hocken, in Berks County. Their leader was John Conrad
Weiser, father of the Conrad Weiser who became the famous "Indian Interpreter" from 1719 to 1729 and the Indians' friend and protector. The Weisers, father and son,
exerted great influence over their compatriots, and the
son especially held at all times the confidence both of the
Indian population and of the Proprietors.[14]

The account of the German people cannot be complete without mention of the Moravians, who settled to
the north of Philadelphia and called their settlement
Bethlehem. They tended to stand aloof from other
German sects and were friendly and congenial with their
English neighbors. They were orderly, clean, quiet,
decent people—the first in Pennsylvania to attempt to
carry the Christian message to the Indians.

Gradually this great second wave of Germans fan-
ned out north and west of Philadelphia—to Bucks
County, to Lancaster County, and what are now York
and Adams Counties, and finally to the Cumberland

Valley. Benjamin Chambers had not been here more than a year "until Joseph Crunkleton and Jacob Snively settled in Antrim township, both Germans who came from Rapho township, Lancaster County . . . In 1736 the 'German Settlement' at Grindstone Hill was begun; in the same year Germans settled in Green township; in 1737 Samuel Bechtel was a resident of Path Valley."[15]

We may conclude this section by quoting again from the author whom I have just cited, for he brings together our discussion of the two elements of immigration into the Cumberland Valley:

We are citizens of no mean county. . . . Settled almost at the same time by the Scotch-Irish and Germans, the two peoples have become intermingled so that it is difficult now to tell in many instances where one ancestry has predominance over the other. But the majority of our citizens are of German descent. This was not so at first. The Scotch-Irish were the more numerous. They were of the energetic, restless temperament that made them brave and eager warriors, astute politicians and progressive citizens. The Germans made less rapid entry upon the lands. They were as intelligent as their neighbors though not so intellectual; they were not fond of war and fought only when they must; they were plodding and frugal, delighting in rich crops and comfortable homes, and while they hurried forward their material advancement less quickly than the Scotch-Irish they made it much more secure. In the early history of the county they do not figure much except as honest, prosperous farmers. They were not regarded with the same sense of equality by the Scotch-Irish as later, and they were kept in the background in governmental affairs. We have no evidence that they fretted much because of this; they were satisfied to build homes, when they could do so in peace, and establish that solid foundation which they have always laid everywhere in their communities.[16]

CHAPTER I. THE EARLY SETTLERS

The Founder of Chambersburg

Benjamin Chambers was about twenty-one years old when he and his three brothers decided to cross the Susquehanna River and explore the Great Valley to the southwest. They prepared their journey carefully, for no one except perhaps an occasional trader had embarked on the exploration of this somewhat forbidden territory.

They came slowly, noting the hills, valleys, and streams they met. James liked the Big Spring and said he would stop there and try to make his fortune. Robert preferred the Middle Spring and settled beside it. Joseph and Benjamin, the youngest of the four, pressed on. They could have settled with their brothers, but like so many of the Scotch-Irish they instinctively wanted independence and a place of their own. So they pushed on, following an Indian trail—the only kind of road then in existence in the Valley.

They arrived at a place where one body of water flowed into another. They marvelled both at the beauty of the site and at the proportion of the waterfall. What we now call the Falling Spring had a thirty-foot fall into the Conococheague in those years. It looked like a perfect situation for a water-powered mill. Many years later, Edward Shippen considered building a mill on the Conodoguinet in the town that bears his name. With this thought in mind, he wrote from Lancaster to Mr. and Mrs. Burd on 4 September 1753: "As you go along the road to Virginia, you may take notice of Ben Chambers' saw mill which does without any dam at all; a glorious thing formed by nature".[1]

And so Joseph and Benjamin decided that they would settle here. After a short time Joseph returned, by agreement among the brothers, to Fishing Creek on the Susquehanna to care for the joint property there. Benjamin fell to work, cleared some land around the confluence of the streams, and built a modest house of logs. He would build a mill like the mill at Fishing Creek.*

But he did not build his house or his mill until he had first estimated the future of this broad valley. Would others come behind him? Would a mill be profitable? Who would grow the grain?—who would buy it? Or would he be left alone, a solitary first settler without companions—with two brothers near by also solitary settlers?

Soon enough he had his answer. Within a year there were German settlers in what is now Antrim township. Other Scotch-Irish came behind the four brothers. The Conococheague Settlement began to grow and take a recognizable shape with settlements both to the east and to the west. The great immigration into the Cumberland Valley had begun; and Benjamin Chambers chuckled to think that he and his brothers had been the first to come, the first men to see the tide of the future in this part of the colony. It is true that a Frenchman, Jacques LeTort, lived at Beaver Pond, near the future Carlisle, as early as 1720, but he was more trader than settler.

He turned then from clearing the land to building a mill. The other newcomers were growing grain—only small acreages at first but considerable areas by 1745, and they were grateful to have a mill to turn the grain into flour. But they needed more than flour: they needed dressed logs and finished planks for their houses. Thus came Benjamin Chambers's saw mill, also using water

*Appendix A

31

power from the Falling Spring.

Throughout this early development of his little settlement, Benjamin Chambers was to his neighbors the local miller. The miller in the first settlements was a very important person.

> The owners and operators of these mills, as the records show, were men of intelligence and means, and therefore had much to do with forming and strengthening public opinion. They were not only respected at home but known in the province, some of them in the colonies at large, and their influence was felt in civil and religious assemblies. . . . The church on the Sabbath and the tavern and mill on the week days were the places where the neighbors met and had opportunity to gather and disseminate the news of the country, discuss matters of general and public interest and form their opinions. We readily see why these millers were the men of business, around whom centered the affairs regarding the welfare of their communities. And yet at this distant day it is not easy to grasp a full knowledge of the influence they enjoyed and the great power they wielded.[2]

Thus Benjamin Chambers gradually emerged as a leading citizen of the Cumberland Valley. We know that, after the burning of his first house (for the nails he had used in building it, tradition says), he built a second, two stories high, of stone. This was indeed a mansion by the standards of the frontier. He was also a leading power in establishing a Presbyterian church on his own land and was a trustee of it from its inception. In the years ahead, as we shall see, he played a prominent role in the military life of the Valley.*

*Appendix B

Land Titles and Border Disputes

Until the Indians burst in upon them in the 1750's and 1760's, the great concern of the early immigrants in the southern part of Pennsylvania was the title to their new property. The Penns had said in effect, "Come! There is land, thousands of acres of it. Take it, live on it, improve it. It is yours." But it was not so simple as that. When the Chambers brothers settled in the Cumberland Valley like three robins nesting near one another they were really illegal squatters in the eyes of the law.

The Royal Charter that William Penn received from Charles II on 4 March 1681 made him sole owner of thousands of acres in the New World.

> Besides being the political governor of the province, Penn was also the feudal lord and owner of all the land. It was his intention to sell it to the settlers from time to time in such tracts as should be convenient, reserving on the tracts sold a small quit-rent to be paid to him and his heirs forever. Some lands were sold for a price in addition to the quit-rent, and others for the quit-rent alone. It was a pleasant arrangement for the proprietor and governor; for although neither the selling-price nor the rent was very large, yet when forty thousand square miles had been sold in this way, the governor would be a very rich man, not only in capital, but in yearly income.
>
> The reservation of rent to be paid forever fortified him in his position of lord of the manor, and made all the colonists his tenants. It was thoroughly feudal, and always a cause of more or less dissatisfaction among the people, but not so much as might be expected; for the proprietors were

on the whole not disliked . . . Pennsylvania was not only the greatest proprietary province in point of size, but it was also the most successful one. The proprietorships in Maine, New Hampshire, and the Carolinas were utter failures. Maryland was only partially successful; it was never very remunerative, and the crown deprived the Baltimores of their control of it for over twenty years. But William Penn was deprived of his province by William III. for only about two years; and except for that short time he and his sons held their province down to the American Revolution of 1776, a period of ninety-four years.[3]

The order from on high to the deputy governors was to treat with the Indians in a friendly, honest way. Thus agreements were entered into by both parties about land—the Indians and the Proprietors (often called Proprietaries). Early agreements permitted white settlement east of the Susquehanna River, but not west. Hence when Benjamin Chambers discovered the pretty waterfall on the Conocoheague about 1730 and set up housekeeping there, he was invading land that still belonged to the Delawares. One doubts that he realized this fact at the time or would have been much bothered by it, but it was brought home to him in an unexpected way.

The Proprietors were not blind. Through their Secretary, Richard Peters, they knew what was happening in the Cumberland Valley and elsewhere in their domain. They also knew that the province of Maryland was eager to send settlers into this territory so as to establish a property right; and for this reason the Proprietors were quite willing to have immigrants like the

Chambers brothers push into the disputed territory as a means of establishing their 'right' to the area. Possession was then nine-tenths of the law even more emphatically than it is now.

So no one told the Chambers brothers to leave. Benjamin continued to expand his modest holding; and when he learned that there was a semi-legal way of assuring his land title, he seized upon it. What was it? It was a splendid frontier subterfuge.

The Proprietors were bent upon having their own people come to these lands as a counterweight to penetration by Marylanders. So, pending a purchase agreement with the Delawares and pending a settlement of the borderline with Maryland, the Proprietors authorized a man named Samuel Blunston, a magistrate of Lancaster, to issue 'licenses' to settlers west of the Susquehanna. They were not 'titles' and could not be until there was a land agreement with the Delawares. Benjamin Chambers received a 'Blunston license' for his Concocheague Settlement on 30 March 1734.[4] At last he breathed easy. It was now unlikely that anyone would seek to evict him. It was from this date that he began in earnest the development of his holding, confident of his possession of it. It is interesting that he did not receive a 'patent', *i.e.*, a full and defensible title to his land, until 1742. By that date he was beyond any doubt about his possession of his property. Time and success had sealed it.

Pennsylvania had three border disputes in the first century of her existence: one with Virginia over the western counties; another with Connecticut over the northern tier; and a third with Maryland. The first two lie outside the scope of this account, but the third is of cardinal importance to it. The Pennsylvania-Maryland dispute might be called a cartographers' quarrel.

The cause of the contention dates back to the time of King James I of England when in 1606 he granted to the London Company four degrees of latitude on the Atlantic from the 34th to the 38th parallel; and to the Plymouth Company four degrees from the 41st to the 45th parallel, leaving three degrees from 38 to 41 as neutral or common territory. Within these three degrees King Charles I in 1632 granted to Lord Baltimore the territory lying under the 40th degree of north latitude while the grant to William Penn in 1681 by King Charles II was limited on the south by the beginning of the said 40th degree, thus making an overlap of one whole degree. Note the language—Lord Baltimore's grant reads *under* the 40th degree of latitude while Penn's grant reads to the *beginning* of the 40th degree. It should be borne in mind that a degree of latitude is not an invisible line, but a definite space or belt upon the earth's surface of approximately 69-1/2 miles. Here then was the cause of their principal contention. . . . had Lord Baltimore's contention been sustained most of the built-up portion of Philadelphia would have belonged to him. On the other hand had Penn's contention prevailed the city of Baltimore itself would have been in Pennsylvania territory . . .

Penn's grant was also the only one limited by longitude. He was given five degrees, but he could just as easily have had it reach to the Pacific Ocean. . .

In making these grants, history says that a map

made in 1614, by Captain John Smith of Pocahontas fame, was used. It was believed to be correct, but in 1682 it was discovered that the true meridian of 40 degrees was nineteen miles north of where Captain Smith located it. By that map the 40 degree line is laid down as crossing the Delaware River where the city of Newcastle now stands. Penn was deeply disappointed, Lord Baltimore was highly elated, and the controversy between the provinces, thus lying side by side, was waged with spirit and varying results between Lords Baltimore and the Penn family from 1682 to 1767.[5]

The later of these two years is the date of completion of the Mason-Dixon Line. Meanwhile some agreement was urgently needed: settlers were coming rapidly and wanted to hold secure titles to their lands. Were they in Pennsylvania or were they in Maryland? And so in 1732 the two provinces agreed to run a Temporary Line that could serve as a boundary until a permanent line could be properly surveyed.

> More border troubles occured in the decade between 1740 and 1750 than during any previous or subsquent time. The Temporary Line which had been agreed to by the Proprietaries in 1732 was not run and finally determined until 1738. This unsettled condition of affairs . . . caused an endless amount of trouble for a period of more than 40 years.[6]

Benjamin Chambers was drawn into this border dispute twice, in different ways. These were young Chambers's courting days. He had made the acquaintance of a certain Miss Sarah Patterson, second daughter of James and Susanne Patterson who lived on the Susquehanna River in York County. Patterson was engaged in trade with the Indians near by and was a man of some substance, owning two plantations and many horses. Moreover—and this is the point—his lands lay in the disputed area and were claimed by both Pennsylvania and Maryland.

Patterson was an ardent partisan of the Penns and wanted nothing to do with the Marylanders. But a very energetic man named Thomas Cresap was pressing the Maryland claim and tried to oust Patterson. It was into this personal quarrel that Benjamin Chambers was drawn. Our local historian, G. O. Seilhamer, has left a dramatic account of the incident.

> The conflict lasted from 1732-1736, when Cresap was seized and the Maryland intruders, as they were called, overcome. In the meantime James Patterson, the elder, died, and the work of resisting Cresap's aggressions fell largely upon James Patterson, the younger, and Benjamin Chambers . . .
>
> In May, 1736, Chambers was at the house of John Wright, Jr., on the west side of the Susquehanna, where Wrightsville now stands. While there he witnessed an attempt by one Franklin to make a survey of a part of the great Springettsbury Manor, in York County, protected by Cresap and twenty men under his command. . . . Later, in the year, he was able to perform a very important service to the Proprietary of Pennsylvania in resisting the designs of the Marylanders. . . .
>
> When Col. Rigby, who was in command of one of the Maryland regiments, appointed a general muster in 1736, "in order to draught a large number

of the Melisha to go up to Cadores and Conedeuhela Settlement to Distrain for Levies, that they were pleased to charge to the inhabitants there", Chambers, in his own language, was "chosen to go a Spy to bring an account of their proceedings". He went down the east side of the Susquehanna, crossing at Rock Run ferry, a few miles above Port Deposit.

On this journey Chambers was well mounted, and pretended that he had come from "the Fawling Spring on Cannogogige in Lancaster county", in search of a servant who had run away. When he reached Colonel Rigby's neighborhood, he learned that Cresap had gone to Col. Hall's to meet the Governor of Maryland, who was to be at the muster. This gave him great uneasiness, as he had been one of the persons that went to stop Cresap and the party of surveyors, "who were chaining up the River side on John Wright's land".

The interview between Chambers and Col. Rigby was a lively one, Rigby half suspecting the real character of the young horseman, and Chambers doing his little song and dance about the runaway servant from "Fawling Spring on Cannogogige" with great spirit. In spite of his glib story Rigby determined to detain him, and as a consequence of the dentention Chambers learned that a hundred men—twenty out of each company in the regiment—were to rendezvous at Wright's Ferry on a certain day. This was the information he had come to seek, and having obtained it he was eager to get away. By more smooth talk he induced Rigby to dismiss him for the night as an honest man, the

Governor not having arrived. Going home with one of the militia, he prevailed upon his host to guide him to the York Barrens, six miles away, early in the morning, and then made his way to Wright's Ferry, where he arrived that night. He there learned that there was to be a house-raising in Donegal, and went there to let the people know of the Maryland muster. Forewarned, the Scotch-Irishmen of Donegal, Hempfield and Manor townships, Lancaster county, gathered in such force that the Maryland soldier thought it wise to retreat without attempting to strike a blow.

"The Hon. Thomas Penn being at Samuel Blunston's, Esq.", Chambers says in his letter to Tilghman, "and hearing how I have managed at Rigby's, sent for me to let him hear the apologies I made before Rigby. They pleased his Honour so well that he told Mr. Blunston he should make me a Compliment for my good conduct on that affair; I told Mr. Blunston that if his Honour would be pleased to do so, that I would Rether have it in land than any other way, and as I was a millwright, and that there was a stream called Seder Spring in the Manor of Lowder, that I would build a mill on it, that might accommodate aney of the Honerable Fameley that might think fitt to make a Contery Seat there. On his hearing this his Honour was pleased to order his Secretary of the Land Office, who was James Steele at that time, and was ordered to be Recorded for a Corn Mill and plantation".[7]

Seilhamer tells us that Seder Spring was Chambers's spelling of Cedar Spring, the name by which the Falling Spring was then known to many, and suggests that through this exploit Chambers received a gift of the lands he had already inhabited. However this may be, he had made the acquaintance of the Hon. Thomas Penn, one of the three proprietors of Pennsylvania, in most opportune circumstances; and this was to lead to an interesting chapter in his life.

But first let us return a moment to Miss Sarah Patterson. She and Benjamin Chambers were married on 24 September 1742 at Christ Church in Philadelphia and in due time had a son whom they named James, born beside the Falling Spring on 5 June 1743. The young mother died a few months after the birth of her son. In 1748 Chambers remarried. His second wife was Jane Williams, daughter of a Welsh Episcopal clergyman of Virginia. Seven children were born of this marriage, four boys and three girls: Ruhamah, William, Benjamin, Joseph, George, Jane, and Hadassah, better known as Hetty.[8]

After the death of his first wife, Benjamin Chambers returned to his native Ulster, leaving his small son James with Masonic brothers in Philadelphia. His purpose seems to have been twofold: to bring his three sisters back with him to America in the expectation that they would help to mother James; and to encourage emigration to America from the country around Lough Neagh where he had lived as a youth. After his remarriage in 1748 and before the year 1753, Chambers and his wife visited England. The chief reason for this trip was to assist the Penns in establishing their border claims *vis-a-vis* Maryland. Chambers is said to have appeared before Parliament and to have been an effective agent of the Proprietors. Tradition has it that his wife had inherited some money and that with some of this the couple

41

purchased two swivel guns for the fort that Chambers planned to build when he returned.*

Some of Benjamin Chambers's Neighbors

Life was lonely for Benjamin Chambers in the first months of his domicile beside the Falling Spring. There were his two brothers at the Middle Spring and Big Spring, but what is now a trifling journey was then a considerable one. A lonely life at the very beginning but less lonely as time passed. Within a year of his arrival in the Valley—or possibly in the same year—Joseph Armstrong struck a few miles farther west and settled near the present town of St. Thomas. Like the Chambers brothers, he had migrated from Ulster and ultimately attained "an importance and an authority . . . second only to that of Col. Benjamin Chambers, the leading spirit of the Conococheague Settlement".[9] He was a cousin of Col. John Armstrong of Carlisle, later to become the hero of the foray against the Indians at Kittanning in September of 1756.[10]

Another of the earliest settlers—about 1731 or 1732—was William McDowell, who brought his five sons and four daughters (and presumably his wife also) and made his home "under the shadow of Mount Parnell",[11] not far from John Armstrong. He came of the "fighting stock of the Clan Argyle". One of these five sons built a mill a few years later at Bridgeport (now Markes) and ultimately turned it into one of the forts that dotted the Valley when the Indian trouble erupted.

There were immigrants coming to Shippensburg at this time—"we have eighteen cabins built here now", wrote James Magraw on 21 May 1733.[12] In another direction, in the Little Cove in what was then Peters town-

*Appendix C

42

ship, there was a small colony of Welsh by 1734, with euphonious names straight from their native land whose mountains much resembled those to which they had come: Shelby, Harrod, Davis, Phillips, Evans, Owens, et al. The children of these people were later to suffer great hardships at the hands of angry Indians.

A neighbor who was to grow to considerable stature in the Valley was Thomas Campbell. Like William McDowell, he too was of the Clan Argyle. Indeed, he had occupied the responsible post of Captain of the Horse of that Clan. He seems to have been implicated in the Jacobite plot which sought to return the Stuarts to the throne; and when that plot failed temporarily in 1715 (the so-called "Fifteener")[13], he fled to Ulster, remained ten years, and made his way to America in 1725. Gradually he travelled west and founded Campbellstown in 1734. This name remained current until 1818, when it was changed to St. Thomas.[14] With Campbell came another Argylshire man, John Dixon; and more Campbells arrived after the last cruel defeat of the House of Stuart at Culloden in 1746. By 1738 the area comprising Welsh Run, Loudon, and St. Thomas was well settled. The meeting house on Church Hill stood at about the center of this area.[15]

In the East Conococheague Settlement, later to be called Greencastle, there was William Allison, an Ulsterman born in 1696, who came to the Valley well before mid-century. He became a prominent citizen and later a magistrate. He went with Richard Peters and Benjamin Chambers on the unpleasant errand in 1750 that resulted in the name of Burnt Cabins.[16]

James McLene, unlike Allison, was born in America, at New London in Chester County in 1730, the year of

Benjamin Chambers's arrival at the Falling Spring. He migrated to the Valley in 1753 and made his home in the East Conocheague Settlement. He was one of the representatives at the Provincial Conference at Carpenter's Hall on 18 June 1776 that met to prepare the way for a Convention that would give Pennsylvania a new constitution which would "best conduce to the happiness and safety of all the citizens". This is the Convention that established the famous Pennsylvania Flying Camp, a body of 4,500 men whose duty it was to move swiftly to meet emergencies. McLene was appointed a member of the executive committee charged with organizing this body. Most important of all, he was a member also of the Constitutional Convention that met in that same summer.

James McLene is next recorded as sitting with the Continental Congress. Of that important body he was an able and active member, during the trying session of 1779-1780. His colleagues from Pennsylvania in the Congress were John Armstrong, Frederic A. Muhlenberg, William Shippen and James Searle. It was indeed a time that tried men's souls. Who can measure the importance of the problems which those unselfish patriots, who constituted the Continental Congress were called upon to solve, particularly at the period when McLene took his seat among them? The finances of the country were in a wretched condition. The doctrine of state's rights in its most radical form was rampant. The sufferings of the rank and file of the army; the petty jealousies of the officers and the secret distrust of men high in authority constantly fostered by the envy of ambitious subordinates and the hidden machinations of the tory element, were enough to fill the days of these single-minded patriots with anxiety and their nights with suspense. Yet, they never wavered in their allegiance and service and the shadow of scandal never fell upon any of their acts.[17]

James and Jean McCalmont settled near the present town of Upper Strasburg in 1737 and in that same year their son James the younger was born. Both father and son served in Captain Joseph Armstrong's rangers in 1755 and under Col. Samuel Culbertson in the Cumberland County Militia in 1776-1778, but before that date the son achieved a great reputation as an Indian-fighter.

He was a tall, athletic man, with black hair and eyes, and of agreeable and unpretending manner. He was a man of agility and of almost superhuman speed. The Indians acknowledged and admired these traits and named him "supple McCamman". They greatly feared him and they desired to capture him alive and put him to a tortuous death for what he had done to them, but they never succeeded and he had many narrow escapes from capture.

He was an unerring shot and was the best marksman in the country round. He never admitted he had killed an Indian, but had often shot at them, and his superior marksmanship was evidence that many a redskin bit the dust.[18]

One day when he was alone in his house running bullets, a band of Indians approached without knowing he was at home. One of them climbed into a cherry tree some yards away and began eating as the others came toward the house. But McCalmont was equal to the occasion. He tramped rapidly on the floor, making enough noise for half-a-dozen men, and called out orders in a loud voice to non-existent companions. Thinking the house was full of white men, the Indians turned and fled—all but the cherry-picker, whom McCalmont calmly picked off with his rifle.

As suggested by the allusion to superhuman speed, McCalmont might be called the swift-footed Achilles of the frontier. One day he returned from hunting to find that a band of Indian marauders had killed several of his neighbors and were in the act of kidnapping his sister. He took in the situation at a glance and was aware that the Indians had seen him at the same moment when he had seen them.

He knew that to linger meant his own destruction. He was already seen by the Indians and there was a whoop as he bounded away. He dared not look back but he knew that he was being pursued. On, on, he ran at his best speed, and it was not until he reached the summit of Boyd's Hill, at least a mile away, that he ventured to turn his head. He gave but one quick glance but it was sufficient to show him that there was a powerful savage only a few yards behind him, with tomahawk uplifted, in the act of throwing the keen-edged weapon. A dodge to the side saved the Major. The weapon whizzed by him, striking a tree beyond, and plunging into the hard wood up to the handle. It was then that McCalmont turned upon his pursuer, who was far in advance of his comrades. Like a flash, up to his shoulder went the Major's rifle. There was a sharp report and the Indian fell. Without waiting to ascertain the full effects of his shot, McCalmont

46

started off anew, reloading his rifle as he ran, and never stopped until he safely reached the fort at Shippensburg, a distance of fully twelve miles.[19]

Nearer geographically to Benjamin Chambers than any of these were the three Culbertson brothers who established Culbertson's Row about four miles northwest of the Falling Spring.

Culbertson's Row was virgin soil until somewhere between 1730 and 1735 when Alexander Culbertson and his brother Samuel emigrated from Ireland and settled in this locality. . . . . A little later Joseph Culbertson came from Ireland and settled on lands near his brothers. They named their settlement Culbertson's Row, after a place they left in Ireland. There is tradition that its name was given it because of the number of Culbertsons living on adjoining farms in a row; hence Culbertson's Row. These lands lie a short distance from what is now Culbertson station on the Western Maryland railway.

Captain Alexander Culbertson was a pioneer by instinct, a farmer by occupation, a soldier from duty and a patriot by heredity. His patriotism was inherited by his family whose services as the records show were at their country's call when "the inalienable rights of life, liberty, and the pursuit of happiness" were menaced. In 1751, the first year after the organization of Cumberland County, he was a grand juror summoned by Sheriff John Potter. In 1753 the court of Cumberland County appointed him as constable of Lurgan Township, in which position he served one year.[20]

These brothers were stalwarts in the trying days of the Indian troubles soon to come, and their descendants covered themselves with glory in the Revolutionary War. The impressive monument in the cemetery of the Rocky Spring Presbyterian Church bears witness to the large part they played in the military affairs of the Valley and of the young nation.

To the west, in Horse Valley. John Rosenberry and his family settled about 1756.[21] To the east, in Buchanan Valley, Thomas and Mary Jemison and their three children settled two years later. They had left Belfast in the autumn of 1743 and had arrived in Philadelphia on 7 October. Their youngest child, a girl named Mary, was born during the voyage. The family had hardly begun a new life on the frontier when a band of Indians swooped down upon them and some guests who were visiting them, murdering everyone except Mary and one small boy. The boy has dropped from sight, but Mary, then a child of fifteen, was taken to Fort Pitt and then down the Ohio River. Here she was adopted by two Indian squaws. She married and bore a son; but when her husband died soon after, she was taken to Geneva County in New York. Here she remarried and had six children. Much later she told her story to a white missionary, Mrs. Asher Wright, and thus entered the gallery of frontier women whose experiences will always be considered a strange mixture of sadness and romance.[22]

On 13 February 1765, Thomas and Richard Penn conveyed to James Armstrong a considerable tract of land near Campbellstown for £36.0.1 and the payment annually of a quit-rent of 1/2d. sterling per acre "in coin current as exchange shall then be between the Province and the city of London". This farm, consisting of 212 acres, later became the property of William Steele, who on 23 October 1779 conveyed it to John Wilson of Derry Township, Lancaster County, for £9,000. Thus did the family that was to produce Sarah Wilson, for whom Wilson College is named, settle in Franklin County.[23]

Most of Benjamin Chambers's neighbors were farmers, but not all. At Cheesetown, three miles northwest of Chambers's Fort in Hamilton township, lived William Furley. He had a match factory, making the old blue-headed sulphur matches which were the common matches of the time in the Valley. He is said to have had a flourishing trade.[24]

In 1734 Charles and Eleanor Maclay emigrated from northern Ireland and, proceeding westward, settled in Lurgan township. We know little about them except that they produced two sons who achieved considerable distinction in the latter half of the century. The elder of these boys, William, was born in the year when his parents arrived in America. Of his early boyhood in the Cumberland Valley we know little or nothing; but in 1758, when he was 24 years of age, he was a lieutenant serving with General John Forbes during the expedition that resulted in the capture of Fort Duquesne. In 1763-4 he accompanied Col. Henry Bouquet on his campaign against Pontiac and the Indians along the Ohio and Muskingum Rivers.

But his fame as a frontiersman and as a statesman in his middle and later years far outshone his deeds as a soldier. In 1771, when Northumberland County was created, he laid out the town of Sunbury and resided there. In 1789-91 he was a member of the United States Senate, where he forcefully opposed the Federalist policies of Alexander Hamilton and upheld the rights and dignity of the rural districts against the interests of the cities to the east. Moreover, he kept a journal during his days in the Senate, a journal that in some parts makes spicy reading now. It has been called the only complete record of debates in the first session of the United States Senate.[25]•

The second Maclay son who enters this narrative was Samuel, born in Lurgan township in 1740 and thus six years younger than William. He followed his elder brother to Northumberland County and in 1795-97 was a member of the House of Representatives of the United States. In 1802 he was elected to the United States Senate and served continuously until his resignation on 4 January 1809.

A cousin of these two Maclays was John Maclay, also of Lurgan township. He was born in 1734, a few days after his parents' arrival in America. He was a farmer and a lifelong resident of the Cumberland Valley; and it was he who built the first grist mill on the Conodoguinet. He was appointed a Colonial Magistrate in 1760 and was a man of considerable position and influence in the Valley. This judgment is confirmed by the fact that he was sent as a delegate to the Carpenter's Hall Convention which met on 24 June 1776. Here he voted a resounding "Aye!" to a motion concurring with the vote of Congress for independence. He later served as a member of the Pennsylvania Assembly from 1783 through 1794.[26]

Not long before the outbreak of the Revolutionary War, there settled near where Waynesboro was later to stand a man about whose name a myth has grown up.

Before the revolutionary days, John Bourns, of Scotch ancestry, was born in Adams county and came across the mountains to this county in 1773.

•Appendix M

50

He was a man of resources and industry and he built his own house and blacksmith shop and prepared to rear a family.

He chose for his home a site on the Antietam creek close by Roadside, not far from a tract of land that formerly was (and probably is now) used as an orchard by the forest academy. He did the usual work of blacksmithing and manufacture.

He was a stern old Presbyterian and a man of influence in his commmunity. And, too, he was a patriot. He did for the American Colonies what no man had ever done before in America.

With his Scotch perspicacity he reasoned that what the American army needed as much as anything else in its struggle with the British was cannon and he set about to make one. He was without the appliances for casting a cannon, so he determined to create one of wrought iron. He made all his preparations and then called in his neighbors. They came in goodly numbers and they came with enthusiasm for they too were patriots, and they wanted to help in this work of furnishing a big war gun to the army of the colonies.

They were busy people about the Bourns place that day. There was to be no cessation of work and the women of the household, aided by some of the housewives of the vicinity, prepared huge and steaming meals for all who were to have a part in this remarkable venture.

Everything was made ready. An extra pair of bellows was set up; a big lot of fuel was supplied; each man was instructed in his duty, and then the momentous work began.

Under the leadership of James Bourns, brother of John, the men pumped the bellows and kept up a continuous hot fire.

John Bourns had prepared a core of iron and as the neighbors heated iron bars to whiteness he took them from their beds of coals and welded them around the core. Never did his hammer ring out a lustier sound and never did it fall with such uninterrupted regularity. He worked without resting. His helpers at the bellows relieved each other, and during their times of inactivity they ate with relish the food which was kept ready for them by Mrs. Bourns and her neighbors.

It was far on in the day when the cannon was finished but it can be imagined that the woods reechoed with the lusty shouts that announced this completion in the forest of a weapon for the defence of their country.

John Bourns then smoothed the bore and sent the cannon to the revolutionary army. Singularly enough the maker of the cannon, who had joined the colonists' army, was present at the battle of Brandywine, when the weapon was captured by the British.

It is not known what became of it. For a long time it was said that it had been sent to England and placed in the tower of London. This, however, has been disproved.

It is of interest to know that John Bourns was a first cousin of Robert Burns, the wonderfully talented Scotch poet, their fathers having been brothers. It will be remembered that Robert Burns was very poor in his earlier life and that he was seriously considering leaving Scotland and coming to America, with the purpose of settling at Jamaica. He had engaged his passage on a boat, in 1786, when suddenly his book of poems began to sell and he procured some money for his immediate needs. With this to make his pathway somewhat rosier, he determined to stay at home.

It is difficult to resist suggesting the query—if Robert Burns had sailed to America and had grown anxious for the companionship of some one of kindered Scotch spirit, and had come to this continent and to this county to his cousin's mountain home, would he have sung here the incomparable songs that long have thrilled the world?[27]

We have already seen that Joseph Crunkleton and Jacob Snively had come to the East Conococheague Settlement near the present Greencastle within a year of Benjamin Chambers's arrival at the Falling Spring. The dual immigration continued unabated, both Scotch-Irish and German. The Valley was rapidly assuming the nature of a community ready to announce its own legal identity.

William Penn in 1682 had marked out three counties in his grant of land: Chester, Bucks, and Philadelphia. As immigration flowed westward, Lancaster County was formed from Chester on 10 May 1729; and during the years of which we have been writing the Cumberland Valley was still part of Lancaster County. This meant that, when a legal point had to be settled, the inhabitants of the Valley had to undertake the long journey to Lancaster. Moreover, authorities in Lancaster were not well acquainted with either the people or the affairs of the Valley. All this meant delay and irritation.

This situation was eased somewhat when York County was created from Lancaster County on 9 August 1749; and it was totally resolved when a few months later, on 27 January 1750, Cumberland County was established from Lancaster County. Carlisle was the county seat; and if one had to ride from the Conococheague Settlement by the Falling Spring to register a deed or consult an attorney, the journey was nothing as compared to the long road to Lancaster. The southern portion of this Valley remained within the confines of Cumberland County throughout all the years of the Revolutionary War. On 9 September 1784, Franklin County was created from Cumberland.[28]

But now, as in the myth of the golden apple, there sprang up immediate and heated contention. Where was the county seat to be? Since the boundaries of the new county had not yet been precisely drawn, the people of Lurgan township favored Shippensburg and were against the selection of either of the other two claimants, Chambers-Town and Greencastle. And so ardent were the people of Greencastle that they sent a petition to the House of Representatives of the Commonwealth of Pennsylvania.

> The Petition of the Inhabitants of Cumberland County Humbly Sheweth.
>
> That your Petitioners have seen a Bill published the last sessions for Consideration, setting forth a Division of said County, and nominating Chambers-Town the seat of Justice for that part of said County which is to form the new one, and fixing the Boundaries. Your Petitioners beg leave to observe that as the Division of the County is Calculated to sute the Convenience of its Inhabitants, the most

Plausible method of Distributing Equal Justice, and giving General satisfaction to the people, would be to leave the fixing of the County Town to the vote of the People; allowing two or more places for the Election to be held at. But least any of the members of your Honorable Body should be prejudiced in favour of the place already nominated, we beg Leave further to observe, that Greencastle a Town laid out about eighteen months since, on the Crossing of the Main Road leading from Fort Pitt to Baltimore, and the Carlisle Road leading through Maryland and Virginia, is equally as centerable as Chambers-Town, there is already twenty houses in Greencastle, and a number more building; it is much better situated to draw the trade of the back countries from Maryland, which at present goes chiefly to Hagers-Town, and is so Considerable as to enable more than Thirty Persons Inhabitants of that place, to carry on business in the Commercial line, the Command of this trade would we apprehend be a considerable advantage, not only to the County, but to the Commonwealth in General.

These observations are humbly submitted to the wisdom of your Honorable Body, whilst your Petitioners as in Duty bound will ever pray.[29]

The petition was signed by 221 men, many of them from Welsh Run, Mercersburg, and other adjacent communities. But Benjamin Chambers had laid out Chambers-Town in 1764. Whether because nearly twenty years older than Greencastle or because more centrally located, we do not know, but Chambers-Town became the county seat.

Waynesboro, later very important in the life of Franklin County and the Cumberland Valley, would have been a strong contender for the county seat if it had been formally organized as a town by the year 1784.

John Wallace was the founder of Waynesboro. For nearly twenty years before the building of the turnpike through this section to Baltimore Town he held the title to the tract of land on which Waynesboro now stands. The particular spot now occupied by this town was known as Mount Vernon . . . John Wallace, the younger, was fighting in the Revolutionary war under the direct command of General Anthony Wayne. . . . On July 1, 1777, John Wallace died and left the land that is now Waynesboro to his son, Robert. The latter sold it to soldier John Wallace soon after his return from the war, February 26th, 1783. December 29, 1797, John Wallace laid out the town of Waynesburgh "on the land along the country road leading from Greencastle to Baltimore thro John Wallace's town". Ninety lots comprised the town. They were offered for sale at five pounds specie per lot on the Main street and six pounds five shillings specie per lot on the cross streets.[30]

Other towns and townships were also being formed in these years. Fannett township was created in 1761. Concord, in Path Valley, was founded by James Widney in 1783 on a tract of 600 acres and quickly became a much larger settlement than we find it now. Greenvillage came into being in 1792.

CHAPTER II: INDIAN TROUBLES

No series of incidents in the history of the Cumberland Valley—except the Civil War—has more fully commanded the attention of historians than the incidents loosely called "Indian Troubles". The early settlers in Pennsylvania were on friendly terms with the Indians. William Penn's first meeting with the Indian chiefs under the spreading elm at Shackamaxon has been somewhat sentimentalized, but it stands nevertheless as a symbol of the good relations that existed between white men and red men until about a third or more of the eighteenth century had passed.

The Indians that concern us belonged to two great families, the Iroquois and Algonquins. They were differentiated by many tribal features but especially by language. As branches of the parent Indo-European stock moved apart—such as the Anglo-Saxons and the Celts— and developed languages very different from the original and now irretrievably lost Indo-European tongue, so these two branches of the common Indian stock found themselves speaking different tongues and revealing different characteristics.[1]

There was always a certain degree of tension between the Five Nations or Iroquois and the Algonquins. The Five Nations[2], while hunters, trappers, and fishers, lived a generally stable life in the rich land between the Hudson River and Niagara Falls. They tilled the soil, built cabins and other permanent structures, and had their own defence works. Every school child has read tales of their bravery, their endurance, their warfare, and their culture.

If the Iroquois were somewhat compact and relatively stationary, the Algonquins were more scattered geographically and more mobile. They were to be found as far north as Nova Scotia and lower Canada, in New England, southeastern New York, New Jersey, eastern Pennsylvania, Maryland, Virginia, and in part of North Carolina. They lived by hunting and fishing and moved freely over the vast terrain just described. At the time of Penn's arrival, the principal Algonquin tribes in his new land were Conoys, Shawanoes (Shawnese), Mohegans, Miami or Twightwes, Nanticokes, and Delawares.[3]

Part of the tension between these two large bodies of Indians sprang from disputes over land. Our own Cumberland Valley, for instance, was claimed by both Iroquois and Delawares; but the Iroquois had only contempt for the Delawares and on one famous occasion in 1712 had called them "women," worthy to wear women's raiment and unworthy to fight. And since the Iroquois hated the French because of Champlain's treachery toward them in 1609 and since they had been honestly and well treated by the Dutch and English farther east, they were well disposed toward Penn and his colonists. The superiority of the Iroquois over the Delawares is one of the most important facts that controlled the events of the late seventeenth and the early eighteenth centuries in Pennsylvania.

As has been seen the Five Nations were the controlling factor in the Indian settlements of the valley, as well as maintaining the peace between the Algonquin tribes and the settlers. From the early date of 1683, not only Penn but all his governors treated with them first for land and appealed to them to control other tribes and carry out the treaties. Fiske, in his *Dutch and Quaker Colonies*

58

states the situation, referring to Penn's first treaty with the Lenni-Lenape or Delawares. He says: "Never the less, it seems to me quite clear that in the long peace enjoyed by Pennsylvania, the controlling factor was not Quaker justice so much as Indian politics. As the 'Long House' was the friend of Corlear, the power on the Hudson, whether Dutch or English, it was bound to befriend Onas, (the Iroquois word for Penn). For the next 70 years if any misguided Lenape had undertaken to ply the tomahawk among Penn's people, Corlear had but to say the word, and the waters of the Susquehanna would soon swarm with canoes of befeathered Cayugas and Senecas, eager for the harvest of Lenape scalps. Practically, Penn's Colony occupied an excpetionally safe position until its westward growth brought it within reach of the Algonquin tribes on the Ohio."[4]

Years before, in 1672, the Five Nations had defeated the Conestogas. Many went west to the Ohio country, but a considerable number settled along the Susquehanna River. When white men like the Chambers brothers crossed the river, the Conestogas were unhappy.

As soon as settlers began crossing the Susquehanna and moving westward protests were made by the Indians as their settlements and hunting grounds were on the west side. In 1730 Captain Civility, the Conestoga chief, voiced the discontent. He says: "Wright and Blunston hath surveyed a great deal of land and designs to dispose of it to others, which giveth me and my brethren a great deal of trouble, it being on our road to our hunting.

We are grieved that Mr. Wright did not mind his word, for when he first came to our parts he often said that no person should settle on that side of the river without our consent, but now we find him to be the first and to encourage others." Again in 1731, before the council in Philadelphia, he stated that "the Conestoga Indians had always lived in good friendship with the Christian inhabitants of Pennsylvania, and that William Penn had promised them that they should not be disturbed by any settlers on the west bank of the Susquehanna."[5]

But this kind of protest was at that time the exception rather than the rule; yet we can see now that the white men in high position should have considered it thoughtfully and asked what lay ahead. Blunston and Wright, however, kept on granting licenses to settlers. If the Indians appeared to be a remote danger, the race with Maryland to send in settlers and stake a border claim was of immediate and overwhelming importance.

Land Treaties with Indians

And now in rapid succession come three treaties with Indians. The first was the land agreement that many had expected and in anticipation of which Blunson and Wright had granted licenses.

On the 11th of October, 1736, the chiefs of the Six Nations met in Philadelphia, and reviving all past treaties of friendship, executed a deed conveying to John, Thomas and Richard Penn and their heirs, "all the said river Susquehanna, with the lands lying on both sides thereof, to extend eastward as far as the head of the branches or springs which run into the Susquehanna, and all the land lying on the west side of the said river to the setting sun, and to extend from the mouth of the said river, northward, up the same to the hills or mountains called, in the language of the said Nations, Tayamentaschta and by the Delaware Indians called the Kehachtanum hills".[6]

There are two things to be noted here. The first is that the Proprietors made this treaty with the Six Nations although the land in question was for the most part lived in and claimed by the Delawares. Where were they when the treaty was drawn and signed? Did the Iroquois consider them to be so totally "women" that they were not allowed to have a voice in the disposal of their lands?

The second thing is the vagueness and imprecision of the language. How far do "lands lying on both sides" of the Susquehanna extend? Is there no limit to "all the land lying on the west side of the said river to the setting sun"? We can only suspect that the white men who drew up this treaty were vague by design, intending to take advantage of the red man, and that the chiefs of the Six Nations did not much care what would happen to the Delawares whose hunting grounds they signed away.

If we suspect deliberate fraud in this treaty—and it is impossible not to do so—we have clear proof of fraud in the Walking Purchase of the next year, 1737. This was one of the most despicable tricks ever perpetrated on any Indian tribe by white men; and again the Delawares were victims of a 'deal' between the Iroquois and the Proprietors, The Walking Purchase was said to be in confirmation of a supposed deed of 1686 the exact terms of which had never been established. Here is another instance of vagueness in treating with Indians. Now the

61

whites were to have as much land in the rich Minisink, a tract of land parallel to the Delaware River, as a man could walk in a day and a half. This walk would determine the boundary. Let us see how this was done.

The Proprietory agents had advertised in the public papers for the most expert walkers, to make the walk, offering a reward of five hundred acres of land in the purchase, and £5 in money, to the person who should attend and walk the farthest in the given time. The walkers desired, entered on this novel race on time, through the woods, and though supplied with refreshments at points, without rest or loss of time, one of the white men sank down exhausted, under the effort, and one only was able to continue until the exhaustion of the time.[7]

The Delawares had sent some of their young men as umpires on the walk, but they all gave up either in weariness or in disgust.

The Indians were furious at this crude deception. They never forgot it or forgave it; this we must remember when trouble breaks loose in the Cumberland Valley twenty years later. It was at least with the tacit consent of the three Proprietors, sons of William Penn, that this infamous act was committed; and it is one of the cruel ironies of history that the wrath of the Delawares was later poured out upon the guiltless frontiersmen of our Valley while the men of Philadelphia were spared. One commentator has remarked that it was the blood of the men, women, and children of the frontier that paid for the dishonesty and cupidity of the Proprietors and their henchmen.

For some time the angry Delawares refused to leave

the Minisink lands and threatened force if anyone tried to evict them. Thus in 1742 the Proprietors appealed to the Six Nations to exercise control over the Delawares and execute the terms of the Purchase. This they did in summary fashion, reviling the Delawares in harsh and insulting terms, and sending them off to "Wyomen or Shamokin."[8]

Thus the years 1736, 1737, and 1742 were bad years for the Delawares. They withdrew from their former land, nursing a bitter grievance against the Iroquois and against white men in general. We shall see that they could do little against the power of the Six Nations but much indeed against white men.

Meanwhile in the Cumberland Valley the already steady flow of immigration continued unabated. The tiny settlements of the 1730's became the small towns of the 1740's. Grist mills and churches—the two most distinctive buildings of the Valley except for the ubiquitous log cabin—multiplied rapidly. Farms flourished both on the slate lands near the western mountains and on the less hospitable but good soil of the limestone areas to the east. There was always a supply of game in the mountains, plenty of pure water in the springs and the streams, and an equable climate that favored agriculture and cattle-raising.

> Though the frontier of the Province, it increased rapidly, and in 1750 had about 1000 taxables, its population being five or six thousand. Nine-tenths of the population were natives of Ireland or Scotland.[9]

But the Indians were now showing fits of temper. In this same year, 1750, some of their chiefs came to

Philadelphia to demand 'presents', even destroying on their way the property of Conrad Weiser, the official interpreter and their good friend, out of a mindless rage against the whites. It was perhaps this experience that led the Proprietors to listen more carefully than they usually did to the complaints of the Indians that white settlers were pushing west of the Kittochtinny mountains, then the accepted boundary of the white man's penetration.

Almost certainly stung in their consciences, the Proprietors decided to act upon this complaint. They sent their Secretary, Richard Peters (for whom Peters township is named), to the Cumberland Valley, where he was joined by a group of magistrates, Benjamin Chambers among them. This band crossed the mountain to a small new settlement on 28 May 1750. They called the inhabitants together, explained to them that their presence in this place was in contravention of an agreement with the natives, and burned their cabins. Thus was Burnt Cabins born.

This must have been a hard moment for everyone. For those who were evicted it was a cruel and unexpected blow. They felt virtuous for opening up new land and pushing what they thought of as civilization one step farther into the wilderness. For those who had to deliver the blow it was a most distasteful duty. For distasteful it was; and it speaks well for the respect for law which the leading men of the Valley exhibited that they were willing to undertake this errand at all. The evicted settlers were mostly Scotch-Irish like most of those who ejected them and burnt their homes. They had, after all, gone only a few more miles into the hinterland than Peters's men. They had met the trials of the new continent exactly as the men from a few miles eastward had done. And now they were refugees. But the Proprietors had shown their good faith toward the Indians this time, and this act went some way toward mollifying them. Richard Peters, in writing about this event to Governor James Hamilton, showed his own kind heart and made somewhat light of the destruction.

> Finding such a general submission . . . there was no kindness in my power which I did not do for the offenders; I gave them money where they were poor and telling them they might go directly on any part of the two millions of acres lately purchased of the Indians; and where the families were large, as I happened to have several of my own plantations vacant, I offered them to stay on them rent free, till they could provide for themselves; then I told them that if after all this lenity and good usage, they would dare to stay after the time limited for their departure, no mercy would be shewed them but that they would feel the rigor of the law.

> It may be proper to add, that the cabins or log houses which were burnt, were of no considerable value; being such as the country people erect in a day or two and cost only the charge of an entertainment.

July 2nd, 1750   Richard Peters[10]

Yet anyone living in the Cumberland Valley in the late 1740's would have been a fool if he had not known in his heart that trouble lay ahead with the Indians, agreements or no agreements. There had not yet been any outbreak of hostilities; indeed, these were peaceful years in the Valley, as we have seen. More evil acts were

probably committed by unscrupulous white traders—
many of them a low lot—than by Indians.

Nevertheless, there were rumblings. Traders returning from Fort Duquesne and other outposts on the Allegheny, Monongahela, and Ohio Rivers brought tales of
French incitement to violence, of French hints to the Indian tribes that it was time they thought of seizing back
their hunting grounds from the settlers now on them.
They ridiculed the treaty that granted lands "to the setting of the sun" as deliberately deceitful. There were rumors—perhaps exaggerated as most rumors are—of
campfires, of the sharpening of scalping knives, and the
fashioning of tomahawks.

As a wise precaution against a danger that had not
yet sharply defined itself, the men of the Cumberland
Valley formed a militia on 22 March 1748.

> The old Conococheague families were well
> represented in the "Associate Regiment of Lan-
> caster County, Over the River Susquehanna", of
> which the pioneer Benjamin Chambers was made
> colonel in 1748. Not fewer than four companies
> were contributed by a region that began to be set-
> tled only a dozen years before.[11]

Robert Chambers, brother of Benjamin, who lived
at Middle Spring, was a captain in this regiment. The
men drilled regularly and laid plans that they would
follow in case of emergency. Their most useful device
was a system of rapid communication so that, if a call
went out, the response would be swift and effective. As
colonel of the regiment, Benjamin Chambers had not
only a considerable responsibility but also a unique opportunity to become intimately acquainted with the men

of the Valley. There were other regiments of "Associators", as they were called, on frontier areas from the Delaware River southward into Virginia and farther. They were in the best frontier tradition: self-organized groups of vigilantes who intended to provoke no one but to protect themselves and their communities in case of trouble.*

Although there had as yet been no concerted acts of hostility along the frontier, even the authorities in remote Philadelphia were aware of mounting tension. At, about the time of the founding of the Associate Regiment, Governor James Hamilton urged Assembly to provide defences for the unguarded frontier. The Assembly, however, was composed predominantly of Quakers whose pacifist principles inclined them against any warlike move, even if entirely defensive in intent. Moreover, the Quakers had a deep-seated dislike of the Scotch-Irish, considering them to be brash and lawless. Their way of placating the Indians was to give them 'presents'. From one point of view this practice was a laudable and peaceable gesture. From another it seems more like a form of blackmail. In one year, around 1750, these 'presents' to demanding tribes amounted to £8,000.[12]

We have briefly reviewed three infamous treaties made with Indians. We must now mention a fourth. It was a treaty made in Albany in 1754. In some respects it reproduced terms that we have already seen in the treaty of 1736. Again the white man received grants of land west of the Susquehanna "as far as the setting sun."[13] Again it was the Iroquois who made the grants. Again the Delawares and the Shawanese were desolated. If these two tribes—and especially the Delawares—had needed

*Appendix D

67

any new incitement to throw themselves into the arms of the French, this treaty provided it. For years they had been grieving and brooding over the loss of their hunting grounds. Now their last hope of redress was gone—unless perhaps by siding with the French they could win back what the English with the connivance of the Iroquois had stripped from them. These sulking tribes were like tinder. All that was needed was a spark.

War Between England and France

The spark was not long in coming. In this same year open warfare broke out between Great Britain and France over the control of the North American continent.[14] All the British settlements of consequence were along the Atlantic seaboard southward and as far as the Allegheny mountains westward. The French controlled Canada and the Great Lakes, and their traders and missionaries had penetrated the mid-continent by way principally of the great rivers—Niagara, Allegheny, Ohio, and Mississippi. Their strategy was to encircle and contain the British settlers by controlling these waterways, thus gaining a direct route by land and water from the Great Lakes to their city of New Orleans. At various points along this route they had forts: Detroit, Duquesne, St. Louis, and others.

The British saw clearly enough that the future of North America hung in the balance and resolved to break this complex of waterways at some critical point. Fort Duquesne was an obvious choice. It was far enough from Canada to prevent easy reinforcement of the French and it was near enough to British settlements to make a campaign possible though certainly not easy. Moreover, it stood in a very strategic position, commanding the confluence of the Allegheny and the Monongahela and facing into the mighty Ohio.

Thus Major-General Edward Braddock was posted to Virginia with orders to capture Fort Duquesne. He arrived in February of 1755. After some months of administrative confusion he faced westward with his 2,000 regulars and provincials and an aide named George Washington.

History has been harsh to General Braddock. The fact is that Braddock was a very capable commander. The British government sent him to America because of his ability, believing he was the man to do the job—a disagreeable but very necessary job. He was not the stolid, unimaginative officer that we have been led to believe him. His tragedy was not lack of ability but lack of experience in the ways of the Indians. He believed that the bright red uniforms of his troops, the drummers ahead and the cavalry behind, and their sheer numbers and visible self-confidence would cow the savages he went to defeat. He had every reason to believe so. He had known nothing but success in his career thus far. Why should he be nervous? He had been chosen from a full gallery of officers to do the work of taming the French and the Indians in this remote place in a remote continent. How could he fail? His whole career promised success.

We know what happened: the narrow pass, the river half-crossed, the whooping Indians, the French presence, the confusion of troops trapped where they could not deploy and fight; the arrows and musket shots; the panic of the horses and of the men; the dead everywhere and the wounded crying for help and the soldiers thirsty for water. It was a ghastly business. And when General Braddock was wounded, the already sunken spirits of his men failed utterly. They left their dead behind them and turned back eastward in disarray. General Braddock died at an encampment near the Great Meadows on 13 July 1755, four days after the battle.

We may say that Braddock deserved better. He was one of many victims of the guerrilla tactics of the Indians—tactics not described or prescribed for in the military manuals he had studied at Sandhurst as an aspiring junior officer; nor had he met anything like this in his campaigns across Europe. Defeat at the hands of savages in the primeval forest of America—total anticlimax. It is ironic to think that, if Braddock had won that battle, his name would stand with other heroes of British warfare.

To the inhabitants of the Cumberland Valley this was more than a military defeat: it was a profound psychological shock. As the broken remnants of the army straggled back with their tales of angry Indians shooting from behind trees and rocks, scalping their victims and stripping them of their weapons, the settlers felt suddenly defenceless and in danger of a whirlwind such as they had never known. Everywhere in the Valley there was apprehension. On 1 August 1755, three weeks after the battle, the people of Lurgan township, led by Alexander Culbertson, sent a petition to the provincial council.

To the Honorable Robert Hunter Morris, Esq., Governor and Commander-in-Chief, and over the Province of Pennsylvania:

The humble petition of the subscribers, inhabitants of Lurgan township, in Cumberland county, amicably unite as a company under the good care and command of Mr. Alexander Culbertson, sheweth.

70

That in as much as we Dwell upon the Frontiers our case is at present Lamentably Dangerous, we being in such imminent Peril of being inhumanly Butchered by our Savage neighbors, whose tender Mercies are Cruelty, and if they should come upon us now we are naked and Defenceless, being in a great Measure destitute of Arms and Ammunition. What would be the Event? And now it is only the kind Providence of God that restrains them; and in these sad and lamentable Circumstances we betake ourselves to your Honor's compassions, to a kind and careful Father of whose tender concern for us we are well assured. May it, therefore, please your honor in your Great Wisdom and goodness to Commiserate our unhappy cause and strengthen our Hands with a Quantity of Arms and Ammunition and upon such terms as your Honor see fit and your Dependent Petitioners as in duty bound shall ever pray ..[15]

There had already been a few unplesantnesses with Indians. What was to come now?

The Terror in the Cumberland Valley

Convinced that something must be done and done immediately to provide protection, John Potter, sheriff of the county, called a meeting of the leading citizens of the Valley at the house of Mr. Shippen in Shippensburg. Benjamin Chambers was among the eighteen men present. After some discussion, these men resolved to construct five large forts:

Carlisle, Shippensburg, Col Chambers', Mr. Steele's Meeting House, and one at William

71

Allison's Esquire, in which the women and children were to be deposited.[16]

This meeting was held on 30 October 1755. Two days later the lightning struck and the Terror began. On Saturday, the first day of November, a band of Delawares and Shawanese, led by Shingas, the Delaware king, fell upon the inhabitants of the two Coves and the Conoloways (or Tonoloways) and killed—according to Sheriff Potter—47 persons. Of 93 families in these two communities, the remainder fled, some to Benjamin Chambers's settlement.[17]

The effect was electric. Word of the atrocity spread quickly throughout the Valley, sped along by panic fear. Col. Chambers on the next day—breaking the Sabbath but with good reason for doing so—issued a call to his Associators to gather at Fort Loudon.

> Falling Springs, Sabbath morning, Nov. 2, 1755
> To the inhabitants of the lower part of the county of Cumberland:
> Gentlemen—
> If you intend to go to the assistance of your neighbors, you need wait no longer for the certainty of the news. The Great Cove is destroyed. James Campbell left his company last night and went to the fort at Mr. Steel's meeting house, and there saw some of the inhabitants of the Great Cove who gave this account, that as they came over the Hill they saw their houses in flames. The messenger says that there are but one hundred, and that they are divided into two parts; the one part to go against the Cove and the other against the Conollaways, and that there are two French among them. They are Dela-

wares and Shawnese. The part that came against the Cove are under the command of Shingas, the Delaware King. The people of the Cove that came off saw several men lying dead; they heard the murder shout and the firing of guns, and saw the Indians going into their houses that they had come out of before they left sight of the Cove. I have sent express to Marsh creek at the same time I send this; so I expect there will be a good company there this day, and as there are but one hundred of the enemy, I think it is in our power, if God permit, to put them to flight, if you turn out well from your parts. I understand that the West settlement is designed to go if they can get any assistance to repel them.

    All in haste, from
      Your humble servant,
      Benjamin Chambers[18]

At last, after a long and unpardonable delay, things began to move in Philadelphia. We do not know whether Governor Morris was affected by petitions such as that from Lurgan township or perhaps by the slaughter at the Coves and near by, but two days after the massacre, on 3 November, he called the Assembly together and requested a militia adequate to afford protection to the frontier. Approximately 1,400 men responded at once, enough to form 25 companies. It was at least a beginning. Thereafter the Province itself engaged in the erection of a number of "Provincial Forts" to supplement the private forts already in existence or under construction. Benjamin Franklin, who was no Quaker pacifist but no lover of warfare, helped construct and command one of these Provincial Forts between the Delaware and the Susquehanna.

During the autumn and winter of 1755-56 the frontier was feverishly occupied with the building of forts. Indeed, never before or since in the history of North America have so many stockades and blockhouses been constructed in the span of about a year. Nor were they confined to the Cumberland Valley alone. The Provincial Government built a string of them from the Delaware River to the Susquehanna, and to the south there were forts in Maryland and Virginia.

In the Cumberland Valley there were at least six whose names we know: Steele's Fort at Church Hill, a few miles east of Mercersburg. The Rev. John Steele placed a stockade around his church, shrewdly combining physical and spiritual safety and—tradition says—preached with his rifle within reach. His was a private fort set up in 1755. In extremity, the Rev. Mr. Steele wrote to Governor Morris on 11 April 1756 to beg for men, arms, flints, powder, blankets and other necessary equipment for military resistance.

> . . . for since McCord's fort has been taken, and ye men defeated, yet forsooth, our country is in utmost confusion. Great numbers have left the country and many are prepared to follow.[19]

Chambers's Fort, comprising an ambitious stockade erected around the principal buildings in 1756. One portion of it was over the Falling Spring, thus assuring an adequate supply of water at all times. Col. Chambers procured two swivel cannons as his principal armament. This fort was considered the most defensible of all the private forts in the Cumberland Valley.*

Fort Loudon, a Provincial fort, was the most important of all the stockades in what was later to be

*Appendix E

74

Franklin County. It occupied a strategic position on the road from Shippensburg westward over the mountains and played a principal part not only in the defence of its area but also as a military outpost and storage magazine for military supplies. It was named for Lord Loudoun (note spelling), who arrived as commander-in-chief of all British forces in America on 23 July 1756. We shall return to this fort later.

Fort McCord, also constructed in 1756, lay seven miles from Strasburg and six from St. Thomas (then Campbellstown), almost under the shadow of Parnell's Knob. Its life was cut short by a violent Indian attack on 4 April 1756, when all 27 persons seeking shelter in it were killed and scalped. It is quite possible that the Indians had been watching this spate of fort-building and proposed to teach a cruel lesson by this fierce attack at the same time that they razed one of the new forts. In any case, this sad incident greatly impaired public confidence in the efficacy of private forts.

Fort Davis, also built in 1756, was the southernmost of these forts, lying in the Little Cove. One authority states that King Shingas and his Indian comrade with an English name, Captain Jacobs, attacked it with about 18 other tribesmen on 29 February 1756.[20] If so, it had only recently been constructed or had been built in the year before.

Since they were so near the Conococheague Settlement and formed so important a part of the chain of fortifications, we should mention also Forts Morris and Franklin (1755 and 1756 respectively) in Shippensburg and Forts Louther (1753), Le Tort (1753), and Croghan (1754) in or near Carlisle.[21]

Let us return now to Chambers's Fort, as it was

commonly called. Here is a description that with inevitable minor changes would fit almost all the forts of the Pennsylvania frontier.

> Around the area to be embraced within the fort a ditch was dug to the depth of about four feet. In this, oak logs or logs of some kind of timber not easily set on fire or cut through and about seventeen or eighteen feet long, pointed at the top, were placed in an upright position. Two sides of the logs were hewn flat and the sides were brought close together and fastened securely near the top by horizontal pieces of timber, spiked or pinned upon their inner sides, so as to make the whole stockade firm and staunch. The ditch having been filled up again, platforms were constructed all around the inner side of the enclosure some four or five feet from the ground and upon these the defenders of the fort stood and fired through loop-holes left near the top of the stockade upon those who were investing or attacking the fort.[22]

This description, however, does not fit Chambers's Fort. His was more a compound than a fort. It is difficult now to visualize it accurately for the very topography of the site has changed. The bed of the Falling Spring has moved somewhat from its earlier position. We recall also the drop of 30 feet, which, more than any other single feature, attracted Benjamin Chambers.

One brief account of the fort is this:

> As the western Indians, after the defeat of Braddock, in 1755, became troublesome and made incursions into the valley, killing and making prisoners many of the settlers, Colonel Chambers,

for the security of his family and his neighbors, erected a large stone dwelling house, surrounded by the water of Falling spring . . .

In order to make the house more secure against the attacks of the Indians, it was roofed with lead. The dwelling and the mill were surrounded by a stockade. This fort, with firearms, blunderbus, and swivel, was so formidable to the Indians that they seldom assailed it, while those who ventured out were either killed or carried off as prisoners.[23]

Tradition says that the fort was larger than this account implies. It had an entrance from what is now Main Street and seems to have occupied most of the area bounded by Main and King Streets, the Falling Spring, and the Conococheague. It enclosed part of the Falling Spring. There was room for a substantial number of people and horses and thus the fort frequently served as a place of refuge during these troubled years.

Benjamin Chambers was proud of his "swivels", but they were the cause of one of the very few recorded disputes among neighbors in the Cumberland Valley. A letter written by a certain James Young on 17 October 1756 states:

In our journey to Fort Lyttleton we stopped at Mr. Chambers' Mill, ten miles beyond Shippensburg, towards McDowell's where he has a good private fort, and on an exceeding good situation to be made very defensible, but what I think of great consequence to the government is that in said fort are two four pound cannon mounted, and nobody but a few country people to defend it. If the enemy should take that fort they would naturally bring those cannon against Shippensburg and Carlisle. I, therefore, presume to recommend it to your Honor, either to have the cannon taken from thence, or a proper garrison stationed there.

Acting probably on this suggestion, the Governor wrote respecting them, to Lieutenant Colonel John Armstrong, who in reply, November 30, 1756, says:

I have wrote to Mr. Chambers concerning the guns at his Fort, according to order, but he thinks by going to Philadelphia, he may prevail with your Honor to let them stay where they are.

In the year 1756, he got into trouble with the Provincial authorities about "His great guns". They were fearful that the French and Indians might capture Mr. Chamber's fort and turn these guns toward other places. Lieutenant William Denny demanded these guns of Colonel Chambers in 1757, and commissioned the sheriff of Cumberland county to seize them. Colonel Chambers resisted the demand, and his neighbors sustained him in his refusal to give them up. The people through out this whole valley were greatly excited at what they conceived the unjust demand of the government. Colonel John Armstrong, writing about Mr. Chambers' conduct says: It is as though he designs to give trouble "as he had the brass and malice of the devil".

Colonel Chambers held on to his guns, and having given bond to try his rights in court, the Government quietly dropped the matter.[24]

Col. John Armstrong of Carlisle and Col. Chambers had many times acted together in the common interests of the Valley and would do so again. There must have

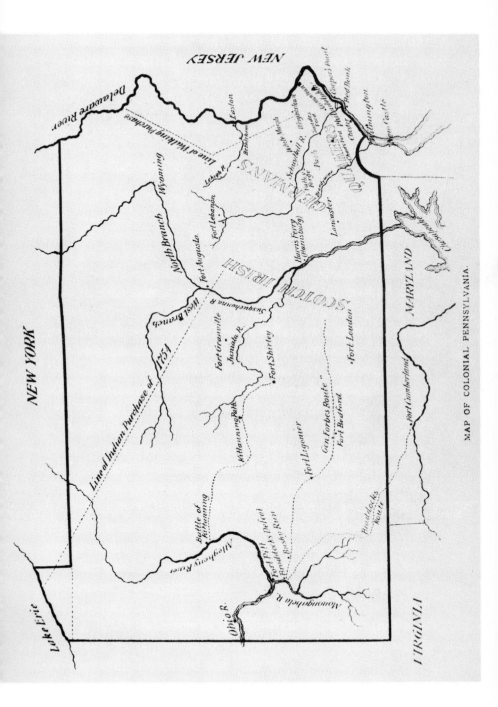

MAP OF COLONIAL PENNSYLVANIA.

been strong provocation to make Armstrong burst out against Chambers and say that "he has the brass and malice of the devil". But, as we have seen, the swivels remained, and it is probable that they, more than anything else, dissuaded the Indians from trying to reduce this fort as they had reduced Fort McCord.

There was safety, then, within the fort but not outside. William McKinnie and his family had sought refuge in Chambers's Fort in the spring of 1757. McKinnie and his son ventured out on 2 April 1757 to visit their land not far away. Both were seized and killed.[25]

Col. Chambers was 47 or 48 years of age when he built his fort. He was at the height of his powers, vigorous, successful, universally trusted. The following vignette tells much about him at this stage in his life:

> Benjamin Chambers had a very good common school education, knew surveying, and was a man of wonderful common sense, good judgement, and could readily read men. He was very brave and was really the chief man of the entire Conococheague settlement. He pulled teeth, stopped blood, settled disputes and was the chief magistrate of his community. He spoke the Indian language and was on great terms of intimacy with the Indians. For this reason he was never troubled by them.[26]

Kittanning

Undoubtedly more protection was expected from the forts than they could ever give. They were essentially defensive. Only seldom did a band of provincials or militiamen go forth, and then only to pursue. There is no extant record of a deliberate attack launched from one of the forts until the fort itself had been assailed. A commentator writing later said contemptuously, " . . a row of blockhouses, called forts, was built along the frontier, with a patrol between them, which was about as effective as stepping stones would have been to stay the Johnstown flood".[27] Another writer has quoted from the historian Francis Parkman, telling us that in 1757 George Washington and Dr. Hugh Mercer went "on a tour of inspection of the whole line of frontier forts. This tour afforded ample proof of the inefficiency of the entire system."[28] Inefficient in the military sense, perhaps, but of immense efficacy psychologically to the whole frontier.

We have seen that the Assembly in 1754 finally acknowledged the gravity of affairs on the frontier and assembled a militia. Two years later it decided that defence alone was not enough and that somehow the Indians should be resolutely attacked and taught a lesson. Fort Duquesne was still in French and Indian hands. It was not until two years later, in 1758, that General Forbes subdued it; and Fort Duquesne was far distant and a stronger bastion than the available forces wished to attack. One had not forgotten Braddock's failure of the year before.

Kittanning looked more likely. It was a considerable Indian settlement, filled with plunder, arms, and supplies. It was nearer than Fort Duquesne and accessible by way of the valley of the Kiskiminetas River.

It was decided to attack this village of Kittanning and wipe it out; and the man selected for the purpose was Col. John Armstrong, a Scotch-Irishman of Carlisle,—the first real soldier the province had produced, and the beginning of the long line of Pennsylvania's distinguished generals.

81

By the middle of August Armstrong had begun his preparations, and soon collected his force of about three hundred men on the Juniata, at Fort Shirley, which was well on the way to his destination. The whole expedition had been kept a profound secret, and was exceedingly well managed in all its details. The men were collected in a way that excited no surprise, and were probably supposed, by most people, to be intended for the usual garrison duty in the forts. An advance party was sent out from Fort Shirley, and Armstrong followed them, with the main body, on the 30th of August. They were lucky enough to make their entire march unobserved. The advance guard came upon the tracks of two Indians, and found where they had killed a bear; but the tracks were twenty-four hours old, and the Indians gone on ahead. If the guard had marched a day earlier they might have been discovered by these Indians and the whole expedition frustrated.

Cheered by his good fortune, Armstrong pressed on, and in five days was within fifty miles of Kittanning. He sent a party to reconnoitre the town, and on the evening of the 7th of September had his force within six miles of it. He intended to dispose his men round the town in the moonlight and attack at daybreak. But about nine or ten o'clock in the evening his guides told him that there was a fire by the roadside, just ahead, and two or three Indians sitting around it. He scarcely knew what to do. It was too much risk to attempt to cut off these Indians, for if a single one of them escaped it would be fatal, and, luckily, he did not attempt it. Leaving a party to watch, with orders to attack them at daybreak, he took a circuitous course with the rest of his men, and reached the cornfield on the edge of the village.

It was a warm summer night. The Indians were dancing, beating their drums, and whooping. They were in the full enjoyment of savage happiness, — plenty of ammunition; plenty of provisions, hunting excursions, and excursions for scalps; and this had now continued for nearly two years. They had received powder and ball enough from the French to last them ten years, and during that time they could carry on the war as they pleased against the whites, who would never dare to cross the mountains. As they grew tired of the dance, some retired to their houses, and others lighted fires in the cornfield to drive away the gnats, while they were composing themselves to sleep beneath the stars. One young buck whistled for his squaw within a few yards of Armstrong, and fired off his gun and cleaned it before lying down. For hours the provincials lay crouched upon the ground among the corn, listening to these strange sounds. But fatigue soon overcame the novelty of their situation, and when Armstrong thought it time for the attack he found most of his men asleep.

Just at daybreak he aroused them; and having given one division twenty minutes to get near the main part of the town, he began the attack in the cornfield. Almost at the first gun Captain Jacobs gave the warwhoop, and cried out that the white men had come, and there would be scalps enough. But his defence was weak. His forces were scattered and soon driven from the cornfield to make a last stand in the houses. Jacobs' house was able to return a hot fire, and a ball from it wounded Armstrong in the shoulder. The sharp-shooting of the Indians was severe, and they seem to have killed and wounded enough of the white men to fully equal their own losses. But the houses were set on fire, Captain Jacobs was shot, and tumbled to the ground in attempting to escape from his attic window, and soon after his house blew up. As the flames spread among the thirty houses, the loaded guns stored in them exploded; and as the fire reached barrel after barrel of powder, the blazing timbers were sent flying in the air. The enemy soon took refuge in the woods, and the victory was complete.

No attempt was made to follow them, nor would it have been safe; and now that their work was done, the provincials were anxious to escape. They were farther within the lion's mouth than they liked. They would not even wait to destroy the cornfield. It shows what terror the Indian skill at bushwhacking inspired, that these men, who had boldly penetrated into the heart of the enemy's country and destroyed a town, were in almost as much of a panic as Braddock's men had felt to get back by the road they had come. By a lucky surprise they had succeeded in scattering the Indians for a few hours, and they needed all of those hours to get a start on their return.[29]

This bold stroke, though it fell on an Indian community many miles away, greatly raised the spirits of the people of the Cumberland Valley. There were other Indian depredations to come, but for at least two years after the Kittanning incident they were sporadic and scattered. Many of those who had fled eastward to York County drifted back, though some remained. And even in these years of fear and uncertainty there was a constant stream of immigrants. Partially dammed up for two or three years by events on the border, they now moved westward in gathering numbers. Life began to return to its normal pace. Crops could now be planted openly in the daytime; it was no longer necessary to plant at night in the hope of not being seen. Out of habit and caution many frontiersmen still carried their rifles with them to the fields and kept a sharp watch, but gradually even this precaution was abandoned. *

We shall never know exactly how many men, women, and children were killed or carried away into captivity in these years; much less shall we ever have a record of cabins and barns burned, horses and cattle stolen, or crops destroyed. The toll was heavy.

Autumn, 1755—Delaware Jo estimated that 200 captives were taken from the frontiers during the Autumn of '55, and of course, most of them were women and children.

July 5, 1755—James Smith, about 16 years of age was captured in the valley.

November 2, 1755—Widow Jordan, and the daughter of William Clark were taken captive near Fort McDowell.

February 11, 1756—Two Delaware braves took two sons of Widow Coxe, John and Richard, prisoners near Fort McDowell.

February 1756—Two brothers, Richard and John Craig, were taken by nine Delaware Indians from a plantation two miles from McDowell's Mill.

April 1, 1756—Fort McCord was devastated by

*Appendix F

a large party of Indians. Among those killed or carried into captivity were Mary McCord, Mrs. John Thorn and baby, Mrs. Annie McCord, and two daughters, Martha, and a young girl.

May 26, 1756—John Wasson of Peters Township was murdered and his wife taken captive near Upton.

July 26, 1756—The Indians killed Joseph Martin, took captive John McCullough (eight years) and his brother James, in the Conococheague Settlement.

August 27, 1756—There was great slaughter, wherein the Indians killed 39 persons near the mouth of the Conococheague Creek.

Early November 1756—Indians killed four soldiers near McDowell's Mill and carried off two, they killed 4 men settlers, 2 women. Persons missing—4 children belonging to John Archer; Samuel Neily, a boy; and James McQuoid, a child.

April 23, 1757, May 12, 1757—Additional persons taken.

June 24, 1757—Alexander Miller and two of his daughters.

July 27, 1757—Mr. McKissen and two sons.

August 15, 1757—William Mason and his son were killed.

September 26, 1757—Killing and capturing.

November 9, 1757—John Archer's wife and 4 children.

May 21, 1758—John Gallady was killed; his wife and one child were taken captive.[30]

Another list, composed in 1811 from memoranda left by the writer's father, indicated that, from 1 November

1755 to 20 July 1759, 197 persons were killed and 90 taken prisoner.[31] But no accurate records were kept anywhere during these years.

If we must always feel some uncertainty about the number of victims, we can feel no uncertainty whatever about the Terror. The Indians' weapon was fear; their strategy was surprise. They never attacked in large bodies, nor were they seen coming. They crept from tree to tree, from rock to rock, always moving silently, always -covering their tracks so that pursuit was difficult if not impossible. The first sign of their attack was the loud war-whoop, blood-curdling and paralyzing. In a way, it was the women who suffered most.

> The annals of the West are absolutely brilliant with the most marvelous exhibitions of female heroism. They had not, like the men, the passions and excitements of the chase, but were left in exposed, isolated cabins, with all the cares and anxieties of the family upon them, and when these homes were suddenly invaded by the pitiless savages and themselves carried off into a hopeless captivity, were liable to see the brains of their young babes dashed out against the nearest tree, and their older children either killed or scalped before their eyes or scattered among various captors. How crowded are all our Border chronicles with the sickening horrors of settlers' cabins attacked and the women and children shamefully maltreated!

> The Mothers of our Forest Land,
> Such were their daring deeds.
> Their monument! where does it stand?
> Their epitaph, who reads?

No braver dames had Sparta,
No nobler matrons Rome,
Yet who or lauds or honors them
E'en in their own green home?

They had no respite from a wearing, consuming anxiety, except in the dead of winter, when the Indians generally lay quiet in their forest towns; as soon, however, as the wild geese were seen steering their way to the north, or the frogs were heard piping in the ponds and marshes, then a great dread came over them. The poet has sung of Autumn, that the "melancholy days have come, the saddest of the year", but with women of the border, it was the Spring whose breezes came freighted with sadness. The customary harbingers of Spring to them were the appalling, blood-curdling yell of the stealthy savage, or the gleam of his thirsting and unsparing tomahawk. They regarded the budding of trees and the opening bloom of flowers with the most gloomy forebodings, and listened to the songs of the woodland birds as but the prelude to the shriek of assault. Then was the bark of the watch-dog at night, especially if their male protectors were absent, far more dismal than the cry of either wolf or panther, since it suggested the probability of lurking redmen, and the fond, anxious mother would start from her troubled slumber, and, with ear attent and head uplifted, would listen, listen, listen for the sound of the distant war-whoop or the rude assault upon her barred, oaken door. Then, perchance, she would fall again into fitful, uneasy slumber, to dream of some murderous deed or horrid scalping.[32]

With the coming of colder weather in November, nerves tended to relax and fear subside. But never entirely until full winter set in; for if there came a brief return of summer weather, the Indians frequently attacked. "Indian Summer" has a pleasant connotation for us now, but an Indian Summer day filled the settlers of those years with dread—and gave a new phrase to our language.

CHAPTER III.   PONTIAC'S WAR

These fears were largely laid to rest by 1760; and when, three years later, France and Britain signed the Treaty of Paris on 10 February and concluded the Seven Years' War, the colonists assumed that a final and formal end had come to their Indian troubles.

Let us pause a moment to see how the Treaty of Paris affected the British colonists of North America.

> Britain's acquisitions under the terms of the Treaty of Paris were considerable. In America she secured Canada, Nova Scotia, Cape Breton, and the adjoining islands, and the right to navigate the Mississippi, important for the Red Indian trade . . . From Spain she received Florida . . . Historians have taken a flattering view of a treaty which established Britain as an Imperial Power, but its strategic weakness has been smoothly over-looked . . . The naval power of France had been left untouched.[1]

It was that untouched naval power that later tipped the scales at Yorktown.

These gains were indeed "considerable," but unfortunately political conduct in the backwoods of America was not so rational and gentlemanly as it was around the polished table in Paris where the French and the British diplomats signed. Three thousand miles or more away from Paris there were Indians who knew little about the white man's diplomatic amenities but knew more than any white man about tomahawks, poisoned arrows, scalping knives, and ambushes. In short, the old hatred had not died, and firm peace had not yet come to the frontier.

Pontiac was the most towering Indian figure to stride across the stage in eighteenth century North America. He had an ability that most Indians lacked: he could plan and organize a broad-based and imaginative military campaign. We have seen that Indians generally were tribesmen. They could unite against Braddock because for a little moment they were bound together by a common hatred of the white man and a common desire to humiliate him, but when there was no such powerful incentive, they fell to squabbling and fighting among themselves, often stimulated to strange hostilities by rum bought from traders illegally. There are records of drunken tribal bouts in which it was common that men died in internecine fighting. There was a certain blood-bond among Algonquins and even more among members of the Six Nations; yet the Indians of the frontier remained tribesmen even when, by observing the hated white man and his methods of providing protection by community action, they might have learned the secret of cooperation.

Pontiac learned this lesson. No one in these years hated the white man more bitterly than he, but no Indian was more astute in drawing advantage from the white man's ways. He was so commanding a figure that he forced respect for his organizing powers and his military genius at the same time that he won only hatred and detestation for his cruelty. If he had been a white man, men might have called him a lesser Napoleon fifty years ahead of time; or he might have been another Washington or Gates in the Continental army.

But he was Pontiac, a man with a mission: to extirpate the white man—all white men—in the ancient Indian territories. He could be suave and smooth when he dealt in council with his chiefs or with representatives of the white power. He was the very kind of person whom Hamlet had in mind two and a half centuries before when he said, "One may smile, and smile, and be a villain."

The principal scene of Pontiac's warfare was west of the mountains and around the Great Lakes. In a succession of raids, skillfully planned and impeccably executed, he took all the British forts except three: Detroit, Niagara, and Pitt. These withstood him, but only by a narrow margin.

The effect of Pontiac's uprising on the Indian tribes along the Ohio and in western Pennsylvania was instantaneous. They had lately been quiescent, but Pontiac's drumbeats and war dances excited them anew. They had tried to evict the white man and had failed. Here was a leader of undoubted power and purpose who would at last carry them to victory. Furthermore, there was the force of habit to egg them on. They had been scalping and plundering for many years. Why should they stop now because of a treaty made in a distant capital in a country of whose exact whereabouts they were unsure?

And thus raids begain again in the Cumberland Valley. The people, lulled by a brief but welcome respite from attack, were unprepared physically and psychologically. The forts had not been well maintained lately; some had even been allowed to fall into ruins, especially the private forts. The militia had virtually disbanded and had not been careful to keep good supplies of arms and ammunition. But above all they believed that the recently signed peace between Great Britain and France had put an end to their troubles. Were not the Indians allies of the French? And had not the French signed a treaty of peace? Did this not mean that the Indians were also at peace with the English? It was a fatal *non sequitur.*

Historians seem to agree that the most notable feature of this last great Indian outburst in Pennsylvania was its utter cruelty. It was as if the attackers were seized by a mammoth spasm of hatred, intensified by the memory of all the wrongs they believed they had received at the hands of the whites and by their memory of their ineffectual previous attempts to oust them. They took few if any prisoners. Prisoners had to be cared for in some way. Scalps could be more easily carried. They left no building or crop unburned, no horses or cattle alive. It was a scorched earth strategy.

So great was the panic along the foothills of the Kittochtinny range that hundreds of men, women, and children fled east, some of them for the third time. Fisher states that on 25 July 1763 "there were in Shippensburg over 300 of these unfortunates" backed into cellars, barns, taverns—anywhere that offered even the poorest shelter.[2] Every other point of safety had its quota of refugees, including Chambers's Fort.

The Paxton Boys

And now occurred an ugly incident in which whites, not red men, were the prime movers.

The background was this. There was mounting hatred of the Indians because of this cruel wave of new hostility. There were few if any people east or west of the Susquehanna who had not lost relatives or property in these attacks. Again, the Scotch-Irish Presbyterians and the Quakers were at each other's throats. The former believed the Quakers to be cowards who would not fight

93

in a moment of danger and fatuously tried to appease the Indians with 'presents' instead of shooting them with bullets. The Quakers considered the Scotch-Irish to be hotheads, ready always to shoot when angered. Benjamin Franklin once called them "the unspeakable Presbyterians."[3]

Swayed by a dual motive, hatred of Indians for cruelties administered and contempt of the Quakers for their inaction, a group of Scotch-Irish known to history as the "Paxton (Paxtang) Boys" descended in December of 1763 on a village of Christianized Conestogas near Lancaster and slaughtered a number of them. By chance many of the inhabitants of the village were absent, and the authorities rounded them up and lodged them in the Lancaster jail for safety. Feeling cheated of their prey and resentful against the authorities for their soft attitude toward the Indians, the Paxton Boys stormed the jail and killed all the Indians.

> The people of the frontier knew that many of the men engaged in the deed were not mere ruffians, but were among the best and most substantial residents who had long and effectively been employed, too, as rangers in protecting the whole border. They knew, also, how much that border had suffered from savage atrocities, and while they heartily condemned the crime they inclined to excuse the perpetrators of it. But in Philadelphia it was widely different. They there looked upon the massacre in some such light as we would now regard it. They—Quakers especially—assailed not only the murderers, but the whole Presbyterian sect with a perfect tempest of reproach and abuse. In obedience to public clamor, large rewards were offered for the

arrest of the criminals, but these shrank not from the trial, but boldly proclaimed the necessity of their act, and defended it by argument and Scripture. So great was the excitement along the frontier that to arrest the ringleaders of the murderous band would have been almost impossible, or, at least, would have required the assistance of a large military force.

The excitement, instead of decreasing by time, daily augmented, but not altogether from this one cause. The backwoods people had always suspected the Moravian or Christianized Indians of complicity in the attacks of the heathen Indians, and several attempts had been made to assault and drive them out of their country. So dangerous became their position that at last, though some time before the proceedings just narrated, the Quaker assembly was compelled to disarm and then remove these converted Indians to Philadelphia for safety. Much against their will, they had, in the midst of Winter, to prepare for migration. Their total number was one hundred and forty. It was in November when the forlorn procession—the aged, the young, the sick and the blind borne in wagons, while the rest went on foot—commenced its weary journey. At every village and hamlet they were rudely greeted with curses and threats. In passing through Germantown they were insulted by an infuriate mob, but, meek and gentle, the jaded pilgrims answered not, but steadily kept moving on, arriving at the Philadelphia barracks in safety.

Here the soldiers quartered there, obstinately refused them admission, and the shrinking, cowering fugitives were compelled to stand in the street for five hours, constantly exposed to a hooting, yelling and cursing rabble, who threatened to kill them outright. The soldiers still persisting in their contumacy, the deplorable procession again took up its dreary march, followed by an angry and tumultuous mob of many thousands and proceeded some six miles further to Province Island and were there lodged in some waste buildings. Here they held their regular religious meetings and remained peaceably until the massacre of the Conestogas already related, put an entirely different complexion on matters. Those engaged in that successful piece of butchery, were soon heard to boast that they would finish this Indian business at Philadelphia. The idea, strange as it may seem, soon grew rapidly into favor. The disgraceful conduct of the Quakers—they alleged—in maintaining at public expense, a lot of savages all through the Winter, who in Spring would be found scalping and butchering upon the border, was constantly rung upon with all the changes.

Meetings were now held, inflammatory harangues delivered, false and absurd reports were industriously circulated, and soon these reckless and hotheaded borderers, finding their sentiments were re-echoed from a noisy and lawless party in Philadelphia itself, began to clamor to be led on to that city. Once before they had sent thither a wagon load of the scalped and mutilated bodies of their neighbors to impress the Quakers with a realizing sense of how they on the frontier were treated by their special pets, the Indians. Now they resolved to go themselves, armed cap-a-pie, and to demand protection. This was, indeed, no empty threat, for a force estimated at from five to fifteen hundred men mustered in January, under their most popular leaders, and actually took up the march to Philadelphia.

The ostensible object of this audacious excursion was the destruction of the Moravian Indians; what political designs against the Quakers lay back of this have never been divulged. Their numbers gathered strength at every mile, and the prodigious excitement which the thick crowding reports of this singularly daring expedition engendered in Philadelphia may be faintly imagined. Terror and confusion were universal, and the city was working like a hive of bees. Even the non-resisting Quakers were aroused to a sense of what was due from their manhood in this alarming exigency. The magistrates were pressingly urged to take immediate measures for repelling force by force. Eight pieces of heavy ordnance were drawn up to the barracks, where the Indians were now confined. The citizens, and even many of the young Quakers, took up arms and stationed themselves at these barracks which they put in as good a condition of defence as possible.

On the night of February the 5th, the mob of borderers were announced as approaching. Every preparation was made to receive them. The whole city was in an uproar.[4]

It could have been a small civil war, but wise counsels in the end prevailed. The Paxton Boys—augmented of course by scores of men whose homes were not Paxton—stopped at Germantown and prepared a bill of grievances and demands "expressed in clear temperate language." There was much talk back and forth, during which tempers cooled. Only one request was granted, the revival of the scalp bounty on 7 July.[5] Richard Penn hung back because he thought it would promote private murder—as it probably did. When the tension relaxed, there was an ironical situation that surely was not lost on the more sophisticated inhabitants of Philadelphia. The frontiersmen, most of whom had never seen a city, turned sightseers for several days, strolling the streets, visiting the busy harbor, and buying trinkets to take home to their families. Thus did an incident that began with murder end with merchandise.

This affair was most unfortunate in every way. It involved angry murder of a considerable number of Christianized Indians, members of a peaceful tribe that had domesticated itself under the wing of the authorities of Lancaster. One reporter of the affair calls it the first lynching in our history.[6] This may be too strong but it makes us cringe now.

It involved also a long and destructive march on Philadelphia during which the marchers shot at horses, plundered barns, and emptied hencoops. They were a raucous gang, and they spread fear and resentment as they passed. The march created a wave of fear and consternation in the capital city such as it had never known since William Penn arrived in 1683. The latent but ever-present Quaker loathing of the Scotch-Irish Presbyterians flared into a veritable bonfire; and when the mob arrived at Germantown and encamped there, many expected overt civil strife.

None of this was good. Although, as we have seen, moderate counsel finally prevailed, the reputation of the Scotch-Irish settlers suffered a very serious setback.

Several historians have based their assessment of the Scotch-Irish character and conduct on this incident because it was so spectacular and because the Scotch-Irish were without doubt the protagonists, the aggressors.

It is wrong to draw generalizations from one or two facts, or even half a dozen. The record shows the name of no Scotch-Irish inhabitant of what was later to become Franklin County, or of any German, who participated with the Paxton Boys in their murders or in their march on Philadelphia. These were peaceable folk. They bore, in all likelihood, more of the suffering and the plundering of the Pontiac War than did their neighbors in and near Paxton, but they murdered no Indians, and they did not march on Philadelphia.

Yet the infamy of this imbroglio was pinned on the Scotch-Irish for many years to come. In 1856 a descendant of Benjamin Chambers, seeking to redeem the good name of the Scotch-Irish, wrote a treatise to which he gave the quaint title *A Tribute to the Principles, Virtues, Habits and Public Usefulness of the Irish and Scotch Early Settlers of Pennsylvania*. He does not exactly try to justify the actions of the Paxton Boys but he makes a valiant attempt to explain them by offering evidence that the Conestogas brought disaster on themselves by their treachery and deceit.

> Under the influence of these feelings, at a time of great alarm and excitement, attention was directed to the parts of the Delaware and Six Nation tribes, resident on Conestoga, who refused to join their brethren in arms, professed affection for the colonists, and avowed their determination to remain neutral. That neutrality was denied, and of part of them was very doubtful. Many outrages were com-

mitted in consequence, as was generally believed, of the information and advice they gave to the invaders; and some murders were perpetrated, which the public voice ascribed to a party under the protection of the Moravian brethren.

That some of the Conestoga Indians were treacherous, appears (says Mr. Rupp) abundantly, from the facts set forth in the affidavits of respectable persons. It was fully believed by the Paxtonians, that what were called the friendly Indians, connived at, if not directly stimulated the hostile ones, in their relentless attacks upon the frontier settlers, at that time. That these friendly Indians were guilty of treachery and perfidy, in the manor of Conestoga, would seem evidenced from a number of authentic statements and evidence, from other credible sources.

The most reliable account on record of them is to be found in the communication of the Rev. John Elder to Governor Penn, Dec. 16, 1763, who was the pastor of a Presbyterian congregation in the township of Paxton, and who was respected and beloved for his estimable character. Mr. Elder, in his letter says: "I thought it my duty to give you this early notice, that an action of this nature may not be imputed to these frontier settlements. For I Know not one person of judgement or prudence, that has been in any wise concerned in it; but it has been done by *some hot-headed, ill-advised persons*, and especially by such, I imagine, as *suffered much in their relations, by the ravages committed by the late Indian war.*"

And in a subsequent letter, from the same to

the Governor, of 27th of January, 1764, it is stated, that "The storm, which had been so long gathering, has at length exploded. Had government removed the Indians from Conestoga, which had frequently been urged without success, this fearful catastrophe might have been avoided. What could I do with men heated to madness? All that I could do was done; I expostulated, but *life* and *reason* were set at defiance, and yet the men in private life, are virtuous and respectable; not cruel, but mild and merciful. The time will come, when each palliating circumstance will be calmly weighed. This deed, magnified into the blackest of crimes, shall be considered as one of those youthful ebullitions of wrath, caused by momentary excitement, to which human infirmity is subjected.[7]

Another writer of the time goes even further. He blames this violence on Indian perfidy and also on what was (to his mind) misguided Quaker policy. Here again is the longstanding friction between Quaker and non-Quaker. The Rev. John Ewing, D.D., is writing to Joseph Reed in London. Ewing was pastor of the First Presbyterian Church of Philadelphia and later provost of the new University of Pennsylvania. Reed was studying law at the Middle Temple and observing the colonial policies of Parliament. These two Princeton graduates were among the most prominent and influential men of their time.

As to public affairs, our Province is greatly involved in intestine feuds, at a time when we should rather unite, one and all, to manage the affairs of our social government, with prudence and discre-

101

tion. A few designing men, having engrossed too much power into their hands, are pushing matters beyond all bounds. There are twenty-two Quakers in our Assembly at present, who, although they won't absolutely refuse to grant money for the King's use, yet never fail to contrive matters in such a manner as to afford little or no assistance to the poor distressed frontiers; while our public money is lavishly squandered away, in supporting a number of savages, who have been murdering and scalping us for many years past. This has enraged some desperate young men, who had lost their nearest relatives by these very Indians, to cut off about twenty Indians, that lived near Lancaster, who had, during the war, carried on a constant intercourse with our other enemies; and they came down to Germantown to inquire why Indians, known to be enemies, were supported, even in luxury, with the best that our markets afforded, at the public expense, while they were left in the utmost distress on the frontiers, in want of the necessaries of life. Ample promises were made to them, that their grievances should be redressed, upon which, they immediately dispersed and went home. These persons have been unjustly represented as endeavoring to overturn the government, when nothing was more distant from their minds. However this matter may be looked upon in Britain, where you know very little of the matter, you may be assured that ninety-nine in an hundred of the Province, are firmly persuaded that they are maintaining our enemies, while our friends, who are suffering the greatest extremities, are neglected; and that few, but Quakers, think that the Lancaster Indians have suffered any thing but their just deserts. 'Tis not a little surprising to us here, that orders should be sent from the Crown to apprehend and bring to justice, those persons who have cut off that nest of enemies, that lived near Lancaster. They never were subjects to his Majesty; were a free, independent State, retaining all the powers of a free State, sat in all our treaties with the Indians, as one of the tribes belonging to the Six Nations in alliance with us; they entertained the French and Indian spies; gave intelligence to them, of the defenceless state of the Province; furnished them with our Gazette every week or fortnight; gave them intelligence of all the dispositions of the Province army against them; were frequently with the French and Indians at their forts and towns; supplied them with warlike stores; joined with the strange Indians in their war dances, and in the parties that made excursions on our frontiers; were ready to take up the hatchet against the English openly, when the French requested it; actually murdered and scalped some of the frontier inhabitants; insolently boasted of the murders they had committed, when they saw our blood was cooled, after the last treaty at Lancaster; confessed they had been at war with us, and would soon be at war with us again, (which accordingly happened) and even went so far as to put one of their own warriors, Tegarie, to death because he refused to go to war with them against the English. All these things were known to the frontier inhabitants, and are since proved upon oath. This occasioned them to be cut off by about forty of fifty persons, collected from all the frontier counties, though they were called by the name of the little township of Paxton, where possibly the smallest part of them resided. And what surprises us more than all, the account we have from England is, that our Assembly, in a petition they have drawn up to the King, for a change of government, should represent this Province in a state of uproar and riot, and when not a man in it has once resisted a single officer of the government, nor a single act of violence committed, unless you call the Lancaster affair such, although it was no more than going to war with that tribe, as they had done before with others, without a formal proclamation of war by government. I have not time, as you may guess by this scrawl, to write more at this time.

P.S. You may publish the above account of the Lancaster Indians, if you please.—Life of Reed, Vol. 1, page 34[8]

From a distance of 200 years or more it is obvious that the murders committed by the Paxton Boys cannot be justified and equally obvious that judgments at the time were warped by emotion and by universal distrust of all Indians. Ewing's opinion is clear. We do not know Reed's response.

The Enoch Brown Massacre

On a summer day, 26 July 1764, occurred almost the last of the frightful Indian attacks. Often as a thunder storm will seem to be receding when unexpectedly the most violent lightning bolt of all will strike, so it was with the Enoch Brown massacre. No frontier incident in Franklin County has more shocked sensibilities than this, and none has received more attention from later historians.

Enoch Brown's schoolhouse was situated about three miles northwest of where Greencastle now stands. The children had straggled in and Brown scanned their faces. One girl was absent, and when he asked the other children where she was, there was a guilty silence. Two of the boys squirmed uneasily in their seats because they knew that she had played truant that day and had wandered off into near by fields. It was also true that they had seen one or two Indians lurking about, but they looked harmless; and anyway there had been no alarms for a long time and the boys suspected nothing.

Then came the lightning bolt. A band of Indians stormed into the little schoolhouse, whooping and swinging their tomahawks. Brown saw instantly what they intended to do. He protested vehemently and offered to let them take his life if they would spare the lives of the children.

We shall never know whether some of their inspiration came from the rum bottle, but their answer to Brown's plea was universal slaughter. They killed and scalped Brown and then the eight boys and two girls in the schoolroom. Only one boy, Archie McCullough, escaped with his life. They scalped him and left him for dead, but he survived only to live the rest of his life as a half-wit. The historian Francis Parkman called this massacre "an outrage unmatched in fiend-like atrocity through all the annals of the war."[9]

Now this is a very revealing statement by Parkman, whose *History of the Conspiracy of Pontiac* (1851) is the classic account of this episode in American history. This massacre, cruel and terrible and ruthless though it was,

was no more so than many other murderous exploits of the Indians along the border. It was at least a clean death for the victims, and none of them were gloatingly tortured before being murdered, as happened many times.

What, then, does the statement tell us? Any man who ventures to criticize the celebrated Parkman when this historian writes of Pontiac and his war must be very careful. But Parkman—we know this from reading his works—shared the New Englanders' reservations about the Presbyterians of the frontier. Like the Quakers, he considered them volatile and impetuous. Thus he had somewhat discounted their trials and sufferings, laying them largely to the natural Indian response to Scotch-Irish transgressions. But suddenly the Enoch Brown incident enters the record. It is clearly unprovoked, cruel, repulsive. Parkman—in our present vernacular—over-reacts and makes it out to be "unmatched in fiend-like atrocity." This interpretation of course does not lessen one whit the horror of the incident, but it is important to understand that the affair, while shocking in the extreme, was not unique along the frontier and was—alas—only in keeping with Indian practices on many similar occasions. Its particular poignancy derives from the fact that the victims were totally innocent and defenceless and that all but one were children. The bodies of the schoolmaster and the children were buried in a common grave, and a monument was erected to their memory by popular subscription on 4 August 1885.

Incident at Fort Loudon

We now arrive at what was undoubtedly the most bizarre episode that happened in Franklin County before the Civil War, an episode that comes as close to cloak-

and-dagger as anything in our history unless it be the Underground Railroad. The Indians were shadowy figures in the background, but this conflict was not one of whites *versus* Indians but of whites against whites. It lasted about a year, and before it was over passions had mounted to a dangerous degree, the rule of law was sadly strained, and Fort Loudon attained a new position in the chequered history of the Pennsylvania frontier.

The Treaty of Paris of 1763 contained, *inter alia,* three clauses of great importance to the colonists who lived near Indians and had to deal with them. The first extended the rights of Englishmen to all Europeans in acquired territories. This meant that all Frenchmen in these territories ceased to be automatic enemies and attained the same legal standing as British subjects. The second set aside portions of land formerly held by the French as Indian reservations. The aim was to allay the fear of the Indians that they would be progressively stripped of their hunting grounds in the future as they had been in the past. This clause attempted to stabilize what had previously been a fluid situation. Having the same purpose in mind, the third clause forbade the purchase of land from Indians without the express consent of the Crown.

The colonists accepted these terms as fair enough, hoping that the Indians would understand the effort to recognize their rights and would live thereafter in peace with the white man. But above all they applauded an act of the Pennsylvania Assembly of October 1763 which prohibited the sale of arms and powder to the Indians. Moreover, traders who did business with Indians were required to obtain licenses from the Governor of the province.

When Pontiac opened hostilities in the same year, the people of Peters township were determined not to be driven from their land again. They formed a posse of rangers called the Black Boys under the leadership of James Smith. As a boy, Smith had been captured by Indians and had lived with them for some years, learning their language, their ways of life, and their mode of warfare. He was something of a romantic figure in the Valley, a forceful and determined leader.

In the spring of 1765, the trading firm of Baynton, Wharton and Morgan of Philadelphia shipped £30,000 worth of goods westward by way of Fort Loudon. The settlers suspected that among them were guns, ammunition, scalping knives, tomahawks and perhaps rum. They were in no mood, after all they had suffered at the hands of Indians, to let more war supplies pass on to them. They noticed also that this large consignment did not use the main road past the fort but turned aside surreptitiously onto a private road where the goods were transferred to pack horses. All this looked very suspicious.

Thus a group of men led by William Duffield approached the man in charge of the pack train, Robert Callendar, and asked him peaceably and without threats to store the goods in the fort until proof could be had either that they were Crown property or that they had been properly licensed for passage. Callendar refused, and a few days later the train, consisting of 81 loads, set out for Fort Pitt. The very size of this train further excited suspicion. When the train arrived at the Great Cove, some of the local rangers demanded that they be allowed to inspect it. Ralph Nailer, who was now in charge, permitted several barrels to be opened; and when no contraband was discovered, the rangers departed and the train moved forward.

But this did not satisfy James Smith. He gathered about twenty of his Black Boys who quickly converted themselves into a band of Indians by blackening their faces, donning Indian clothing, and arming themselves with the traditional tomahawk and scalping knive in addition to their firearms. They overtook the train at Sideling Hill and easily captured it. They allowed the drivers to withdraw unharmed, taking their possessions with them, and then began the long task of searching through the 81 loads. Their earlier suspicions were confirmed. They found blankets, shirts, vermilion, lead for bullets, beads, wampum, tomahawks, and scalping knives—all of which they burned. They also discovered 18 loads of forbidden rum and two of match-coating, but these they kept. In this fracas four or five horses were killed but no men.

Meanwhile Ralph Nailer had rushed as fast as he could to Fort Loudon for help. The officer in command, Lieut. Charles Grant of the 42nd Highland Regiment (the Black Watch), sent Sergeant McGlashan with a dozen men to Sideling Hill. McGlashan returned with four prisoners who had probably had nothing to do with the plundering of the pack train.

Two days later, on 9 March, Smith and a group of armed men demanded that Lieut. Grant release the prisoners and their firearms. While Grant was deciding what to do, Smith's band managed to capture some British soldiers; so Grant released the prisoners in exchange for his own soldiers, but he refused to hand over the firearms.

On 28 May Smith and five of his men saw Grant riding near the fort, waylaid him, and kidnapped him. Still Smith was obdurate; he refused to return the firearms. Smith and his men told Grant that they were going to the Carolinas and would take him with them. Grant thought this was a bluff; but when on the following morning the party headed south, Grant saw that the jig was up. He promised to return the arms within five weeks.

The five weeks passed and nothing happened. Neither Grant, the Scot, nor Smith, the Scotch-Irishman, would give in. It was an impasse and remained so all summer. Some hotheads among the local inhabitants circulated a grotesque appeal for united action, but nothing came of it. Finally in November a body of about 150 men surrounded Fort Loudon, demanding the captured firearms. When Grant refused, the rangers opened fire on the fort. Grant soon ran out of ammunition and had no choice but to release the disputed arms at last. On 16 November he turned them over to William McDowell, justice of the peace. Governor Penn issued a warrant for the arrest of Smith, an act which infuriated the Black Boys, but the arrest was never made. Soon someone with more diplomacy than either Smith or Grant possessed transferred the Fort Loudon garrison to Bedford.

Looking back on these events in later years, Smith wrote:

> The King's troops and our party had now got entirely out of the channel of the civil law, and many unjustifyable things were done by both parties. This convinces me more than I had ever been before, of the absolute necessity of civil law, in order to govern mankind.[10]

This strange series of events has been variously in-

terpreted by various people. Some have said that near
Fort Loudon was spilled the first blood of the American
Revolution. There was blood spilled, but not much. On 7
May, in one of the lesser frays of that year, about thirty
frontiersmen attacked the horses of one Joseph Spears, a
trader whom they suspected of supplying arms illegally
to the Indians. Lieut. Grant sent some soldiers, there was
some firing, and one of the frontiersmen was wounded.
Other blood may have flowed when the settlers surrounded the fort and demanded the sequestered
firearms, but none of the records speak of any notable
bloodshed on either side.

The late G. O. Seilhamer, one of our most inde-
fatigable local historians, calls the incident "the first act
of defiance of the military authority of Great Britain in
America."[11] Mr. R. G. Mowrey writes, "This action . . .
deserves . . as much emphasis . . as a symbol . . of independent thought and action in the Colonies as does the
Boston Tea Party."[12] Mr. Neil Swanson, in his novel *The
First Rebel* (New York: Farrar & Rinehart, 1937), bases
his entire story on these two assumptions. According to at
least two of these views, the American Revolution started
in the Cumberland Valley near Fort Loudon.

Miss Eleanor M. Webster takes an opposite view.
She sees nowhere an act of rebellion against the Crown.
The motive was paradoxically quite different: the pres-
ervation of peace.

James Smith and his "Black Boys" were not re-
belling against either the provincial or the royal
governments. Their efforts to curtail the sale of
weapons to the Indians was a reaffirmation of the
Proclamation of 1763, and of the Board of Trade's
Plan for the Management of Indian Affairs in 1764.

111

According to this plan, all traders had to be licensed and bonded annually in the province in which they would trade. All goods were to be inspected by civil authorities at Crown forts before the goods were sold to the Indians. Baynton, Wharton and Morgan had violated both acts. They were not licensed so that even when the Indian trade had been reopened, they were not able to participate legitimately in that trade. The settlers permitted traders who were not carrying weapons and had the prescribed license, to trade freely. They were not interested in curtailing all Indian trade, but simply in making sure that the Indians could not obtain weapons with which they would be able to attack the frontier until there was some assurance of a permanent peace treaty.

There is no evidence of any animosity between the frontiersmen and either government in the correspondence concerning the rebellion. Any dissension mentioned is specifically concerned with the carrying on of illicit trade with the Indians by the traders, or with the antagonism which was felt toward the garrison at Fort Loudon. Past experience had shown the Conococheague settlers the bitter consequences of permitting the Indians to obtain weapons, and they were determined not to allow them to do so until there was some assurance that the provisions of the treaty would be kept. They were aware of the illegality of their attacking the pack train, but looked upon what they had done as the lesser of two evils. It was better to interfere with the illegal trade than become the victims of the profits of that trade, and their actions were condoned to a degree by the provincial government . . . .

It was a paradoxical situation which can be understood only by realizing the settlers' great fear of the Indians. In their opinion, Baynton, Wharton and Morgan and the 42nd Highland Regiment were endangering the welfare of the entire community. It was obligatory, therefore, that they seek to eliminate this danger. In doing so, they violated provincial law; but they were motivated by a strong sense of right and wrong; and as soon as peace was definite, and trade could be legitimately carried on, they did not interfere with the shipment of Indian goods. A rebellion begun in support of existing regulations, the Fort Loudon uprising got out of hand when leaders on both sides permitted personal antagonisms between the soldiers and settlers to become more important than the control of illicit trade.

Faced with continual chance of Indian attack, the frontiersmen were bound together by their own local law, adapted to the rigors of frontier life. It was the key to their survival, and disobedience to the law was subject to immediate recrimination. The rebellion is attributable to these factors. The actions of Baynton, Wharton and Morgan were interpreted as endangering survival, and it was the fear of what might happen which incited rebellion.[13]

The rebellion at Fort Loudon in 1765 cannot be justified legally. The persons who participated in it were in the wrong. They defied the royal and provincial governments by taking the powers of government into their own hands; and yet by taking action, they were supporting the policies of the authorities.

There is no evidence to show that the people of the Valley construed the incident at Fort Loudon as an insurrection against the Crown and the Crown's representatives. They hardly knew in detail what had happened, except that news of the trouble reached them quickly and they laughed at the discomfiture of Lieut. Grant, whom none of them liked because (they had heard) he was pompous and far too sure of himself. All this seemed far away—as it was by the distance-measurement of the time—and Pontiac had about ended his war, thanks to strong British opposition, and all they wanted was peace, quiet, and no questions asked about the Black Boys.

They had only limited knowledge of what was at stake, of the fears and motives of the people of Fort Loudon and the immediate region. They were called upon to do nothing, and thus they did nothing. In 1755 Col. Chambers had sent out a call for help throughout the Conococheague Settlement, help to combat the common enemy. It is at least interesting that Smith sent out no similar call and depended solely upon his Black Boys for a solution to this trouble. Or did he think that his Black Boys would be more effective than any militia force, trained as his men had been through his intimate knowledge of Indian warfare? This is probably the answer. He went his way, and the people of the Valley knew almost nothing about these troubles until the entire incident was closed.

Looking back over all the "alarums and excursions" of these years, the deaths and the kipnappings, the burning of cabins, barns, and crops, and the sufferings of innocent women and children, one thoughtful writer says this:

In summing up we say that not through the savagery of the Indian, nor through the persuasion and treachery of the French, nor through the reverses of the English, but by reason of the stupidity of the Provincial authorities in the conduct of their land transactions with the Indians, and through the insubordination to law, the land-greed and selfishness of the individual settlers, were the defences of Franklin county made necessary, untold sufferings endured, and in our valley alone hundreds of lives lost and thousands of homes laid waste.[14]

CHAPTER IV.   A DECADE OF PEACE

The policy of the Proprietors and the Assembly was now to push the Indians farther and farther west, thus securing the safety of the settlers in the central portion of the province and confirming the importance and security of Fort Duquesne, now called Fort Pitt since General Forbes's capture of it in 1758. Col. Henry Bouquet was given a body of troops and ordered to deal with the Indians along the three rivers, especially the Ohio. From settlements on that river had come most of the recent Indian raids.

Bouquet was a French Protestant born across the border in Switzerland. He had served in the war of the Austrian Succession and later under the Prince of Orange. While in London, he was persuaded to accept the post of lieutenant-colonel of the newly-planned Royal American Regiment and arrived in America in 1756. He was second in command to Forbes in 1758 and thus came to know the frontier well—and the Indian mode of "open-order combat", which he taught his own troops to use. At Bushy Run on 6 August 1763, not far from the site of Braddock's defeat, he lured the Indians into a trap and crushed them. This was a signal victory which sent the Indians reeling westward toward the Muskingum River in Ohio.[1]

Col. Bouquet's success and the Treaty of Paris of six months before which ended the Seven Years' War put a new face on things for the people of the Cumberland Valley. It is true that the Enoch Brown massacre occurred later by some months than either of these hopeful events, but it was a single incident and did not signal a general uprising as King Shingas's attack on the Coves

116

had done nine years earlier. Indeed, it is quite likely that its coming after these steps toward peace accentuated its horror for the people of the Valley.

At any rate, in the next year, 1764, Col. Chambers decided to take a decisive step. He would survey and lay out a town and call it after himself—Chambers-Town. He had now lived beside the Falling Spring for 34 years; he and his family were established in the Valley; he himself was one of its leading citizens; and most important of all there was at last a good prospect of peace. Was there not every reason to think that a town on this advantageous site would grow and prosper?

Accordingly Col. Chambers ran a notice on 19 July 1764 in the *Pennsylvania Gazette*, Benjamin Franklin's newspaper in Philadelphia:

> Notice is hereby given to the public, that there is a town laid out on Conegogig creek, on both sides of the Great Falling Spring, where it falls into said creek, by Benjamin Chambers, of Cumberland county. Lots may be had on reasonable terms and Firm Deeds granted for them by said Chambers; the day appointed for drawing said lots is the 28th day of June inst., being Thursday. The situation of this town is very good for water and stone, both free and marble, and sand all handy to the spot, and a well timbered part of the country adjoining it; within said town is a good grist mill, saw mill and grindstones going by water. The articles of the town shall be read on the day appointed for the drawing of the lots, and the terms of the sale published by me.

> BENJAMIN CHAMBERS [2]

There is a small mystery here. The drawing was to occur "on the 28th day of June inst., being Thursday", but the notice did not appear until 19 July. Was there some legal reason, now lost to us, for this discrepancy? One writer doubts that the drawing was ever held:

> The times appeared to be auspicious for a border town development, yet the late G. O. Seilhamer in a sketch of the Chambers family opines:
> "Whether the drawing was made is in doubt—if it was, it was confined to the Chambers family. Of the deeds on record for 1764, only one is not in the Chambers name. This was to Robert Jack, Sept. 1, 1764, for the lot on which the bank of Chambersburg now stands. According to the records only five lots were sold before 1775, and it was not until 1778-9 that the number of purchasers was sufficient to constitute a village."[3]

Col. Chambers's optimistic mood was shared by others. Settlers who had abandoned their farms in the days of the troubles were now returning to them and starting life anew. There remained also the steady flow of new immigrants, now gradually swelling as domestic dangers receded. To encourage this movement—and to fortify their financial position—the Proprietors inaugurated, within a year of the founding of Chambers-Town, a new scheme for distributing hitherto unoccupied lands.

> The Penns at that time were owners of all this land and were land poor. It is said they were hard up financially. In order to acquire ready cash for land that produced no revenue to them, a new scheme was conceived in the hope that it would be attractive

to new settlers and at the same time give the Penns ready cash. This plan of selling the land was known as "The Application System." This plan was first adopted on August 1st, 1765, for a portion of the land to the east of the Susquehanna and on the 1st of August, 1766, this system was applied to a part of the territory west of the Susquehanna, and the section thus offered for sale included all the land from the Susquehanna on the east to the western limits of Bedford and Blair counties, and from the Mason & Dixon line northward to the northern limits of Center county.

At the cost of £10 per 100 acres or 26 2/3 cents per acre, land could be secured under this system. Four hundred acres was the maximum that could be secured by any one person. All that was necessary to secure land was to file with the surveyor's office an application setting forth the approximate number of acres desired and specifying the particular tract by some specific and well defined land marks, which would then be surveyed, the cost of which was paid by the applicant. When the final payments were made, patents were issued. This system remained open for applications until the 28th of August, 1769, to which time 5,595 applications had been filed. Upon receipt of a number of applications, they were placed in a wheel, and then the drawing as it was termed was made, each application being numbered after it was drawn, and the lower number given preference in the granting of a warrant.

This was a great inducement to new settlements, and this valley more than any other section, profited by this liberal scheme, and very soon the western part of this valley became well populated.[4]

Roads

We come now to the topic of roads—a very important topic for settlers who needed means of communication in a new and still sparsely settled land and means of transport as well. The first 'roads' were Indian trails. The Indians kept to the high ground whenever they could in order to avoid bogs and marshes which froze in the winter and were treacherous at other times. And because all Indian travel was on foot, their trails were as straight as they could be made. The other 'road' that the Indians used was of course the waterway, and many of their most-used trails were portages from one stream to another.

Throughout even the worst of the troubled years adventurous and often unscrupulous fur-traders had used these trails. But now things change.

With the close of the French and Indian war, dangers decreased and new men with new ideas and capital became interested in the transportation of furs. Horses were now used to transport the goods to the west in exchange for furs, the path was converted into a bridle path and the foot fur trader eliminated. At first one man had charge of two horses which were driven tandem style. Later the Pack Trains as they were called were introduced and occasionally contained as many as fifteen horses with two men in charge, one in the lead and the other at the rear. With each horse carrying 200 lbs. of merchandise it will readily be seen how this improved method of transportation proved to be very profitable and before long great numbers of Pack Trains were engaged in this enterprise, and along with this radical change in transportation came a different class of men with better ideas and with them came a demand for better accommodations.[5]

But we are ahead of ourselves. We must turn back to the year 1744. This was the year when the Great Road was built from Harris Ferry to Williamsport, linking the Susquehanna and the Potomac. There had been trails of sorts linking the three settlements in the upper valley, Carlisle, Shippensburg, and the Conococheague Settlement, but there was little more than a trader's path from Chambers's mill southward. The Great Road marked the beginning of true highway communication in the Valley.

Eleven years later military necessity brought about the most ambitious bit of road-making yet seen in Pennsylvania, the Braddock Road. It was begun on 1 May 1755 as a road to carry supplies for Braddock's campaign. The chief builder was Major (later Colonel) James Burd. This was an immense undertaking over forested mountains filled with outcrops of rock. The trees had to be felled and the stumps removed; rocks had to be hewed out and cracked down into gravel for road-base. Earth had to be moved. And it was all hand-work by pick, shovel, crowbar, and pulley. Two centuries and more were to elapse before the discovery of dynamite by Alfred Nobel.

The builders must have worked very fast, for in a little more than two months they had carried the road to the top of the Alleghenies, 85 miles from Shippensburg. Here they stopped when the news of Braddock's catastrophe reached them. Two men of the Valley, William Maxwell and William Allison, visited the road and wrote this interesting account to Secretary Peters, chief administrator of the province:

121

The road from there to Anthony Thompson's is better than could possibly be expected, considering the mountainous country it is taken through. Sideling Hill is cut very artifically, nay more so than we ever saw any; the first wagon that carried a load up it took 1500 [pounds] without ever stopping. At the time the roadmakers were in great·stress for the want of supplies, but the workmen had a greater grievance than the want of bread—for four days the laborers had not one glass of liquor, which created a great murmuring amongst them.[6]

This road, continued later to Fort Pitt, was used by General Forbes in 1758 and by Col. Bouquet in 1763. It was thirty feet wide at the start, but the difficulties of the terrain reduced it to a width of twelve feet.[7] Forbes Road is the name by which it generally goes.

Long before the Braddock-Forbes road was carved out of the mountains, traffic from the Cumberland Valley to the west had followed a pathway that began at Shippensburg. This was the route: Orrstown, Pleasant Hall, Strasburg, Horse Valley, Fannetsburg, Burnt Cabins, Fort Littleton, and thence west. This route crossed three mountains, and thus inevitably the road was called the Three Mountain Road.

As we know, it was the pack horse that at first carried goods across the rugged mountains. In 1771, by order of the Cumberland County courts, the Three Mountain Road was widened to twenty feet and otherwise improved from Shippensburg to Cessna's Gap near Strasburg; and in 1784 it was extended westward, leading finally to Fort Pitt.[8] The improvements of 1784 must have been a blessing to the traveller. In the year before a merchant of Carlisle, John Wilkins, wrote in his autobiography that he left Carlisle "about the middle of October, 1783, with the wagons, on foot, with a light gun in my hand, and arrived in Pittsburgh the 10th of November following."[9] It was not a trip to be undertaken lightly. Later this road was much used by drovers who with their cattle could average about ten miles a day.

Roads were useful not only for commerce but also for churchgoing. The early churches were built of logs, very simple structures. Not only did they house the worshippers but they also stood as symbols of the religion that the frontier people brought with them. A typical example is the Presbyterian Church of the Falling Spring, which takes 1734 as the date of the organization of the congregation. The first building was a structure of hewn logs, with doors in the east and the south, erected in 1737. When it was outgrown, it was replaced by a similar building of the same construction but larger, 35 feet by 70 feet; and after the turn of the century the present church was built.[10]

This story of a modest beginning and then a larger structure for a growing congregation was repeated many times throughout the Valley: at Rocky Spring, Middle Spring, Welsh Run, the West Conococheague Settlement, etc. Nor was it confined to the Scotch-Irish population. We have seen already that Germans settled early at Grindstone Hill and near the present site of Greencastle. Soon they also had their churches. One of the earliest clergymen to minister to the people of the Lutheran and Reformed Churches was the Rev. John George Boger, who lived at Conewago near Hanover from 1765 until 1770 and came regularly over South Mountain to hold services.[11]

A Lutheran church, now known to us as the First

Evangelical Lutheran Church, was founded in Chambersburg in 1770, and ten years later Col. Chambers and his wife conveyed to it a plot of ground, stating that it should be "for the building of a Lutheran Church in the town of Chambersburg and the lot to be for no other use than the house of worship and a burying place or other seminaries of learning."[12] In the same year, 1780, Col. Chambers and his wife also gave a plot of ground to the Reformed congregation. The present Reformed Church and graveyard stand on this land.

Col. Chambers had conveyed to the Falling Spring Presbyterian Church on 1 January 1768 the land on which the present church and burying-ground are situated. In doing so he asked only that one rose be given annually in June as rent to him and his wife or to their descendants. This same "rose rent" clause was incorporated also in the deeds to the Lutheran and Reformed congregations. It is undoubtedly true that Chambersburg is unique in having three "rose rent" churches within its bounds.

Churchgoing was a serious matter in the early days of the Valley. Attendance was noted, especially attendance at a communion service, and admission to holy communion was sometimes denied for wrongdoing. But if the sermons were long and the seats were hard, there were compensations. Families often had to make long journeys on foot or by horse to attend services, and so they generally made a day of it. They brought picnic lunches which they ate under the trees when the weather was good. Around the church, or in it, people met their neighbors, exchanged news about families or crops, and probably gossiped as they did so. In more ways than one the church was the center of their lives.

In these years it was apparently not the custom to hold weddings in churches—certainly not in the backwoods. They were held in the bride's home. The groom and his companions walked in their best attire toward the bride's home, but at a signal they fell to racing one another for "Black Betty." This was a bottle of whiskey which the winner held up proudly, drank from, and then passed to his companions. There was dancing until morning and much hilarity. At a certain time in the evening the bride and groom were put to bed and then awakened about midnight and forced to eat and drink whether they wished to or not. And it was a community affair. There were few invitations and everyone was welcome to come. To people whose lives were generally marked by frugality and decorum a wedding was a gala affair.

Apparently, however, there was another way to arrange a wedding in the days when clergymen were few. The Scotch-Irish had an almost mystical feeling toward streams. There was something sacred, elemental, numinous about them. When Col. Samuel Culbertson swore in his Revolutionary troops, he bound them to their oath of loyalty by shaking hands across a stream. And a man might marry a woman by carrying her across a stream. There was a jingle that ran:

> Three times carried o'er the brook
> Is good as married by the book.[13]•

Finery such as one had was in order at a wedding, but the daily clothing of the frontiersman was very different.

The hunting shirt was universally worn by the men. This was a kind of loose frock, reaching half

•Appendix G

way down the thighs, with large sleeves, open before, and so wide as to lap over a foot or more when belted. The cape was large and sometimes handsomely fringed with a raveled piece of cloth of a different color from that of the hunting shirt itself. The bosom of this shirt served as a wallet to hold a chunk of bread, cakes, jerk, tow for wiping the barrel of the rifle, or any other necessary for the hunter or warrior. The belt, which was always tied behind, answered several purposes besides that of holding the dress together. In cold weather, the mittens, and sometimes the bullet-bag, occupied the front part of it. To the right side was suspended the tomahawk, and to the left the scalping knife in its leathern sheath.

The hunting shirt was generally made of linsey; sometimes of coarse linen, and a few of dressed deer skins. These last were very cold and uncomfortable in wet weather. The skirt and jacket were of the common fashion. A pair of drawers or breeches and leggins were the dress of the thighs and legs; a pair of moccasins answered for the feet much better than shoes, and were made of dressed deer skin. They were mostly made out of a single piece, with a gathering seam along the top of the foot, and another from the bottom of the heel, without gathers, as high as the ankle joint, or higher. Flaps were left on each side to reach some distance up the leg, and were adapted to the ankle and lower part of the leg by thongs of deer skin, so that no dust, snow or gravel could find its way within.

The moccasins in general use cost but a few hours of labor to fashion and were done by a moccasin awl made from the back spring of an old clasp knife. This awl, with its buck-horn handle,.was an appendage of every bullet-pouch strap, together with a roll of buckskin thongs for mending moccasins, which was the labor of almost every evening. They were sewed and patched together with deerskin thongs, or whangs, as they were commonly called. In cold weather, these moccasins were well stuffed with deer's hair or dry leaves, so as to keep the feet comfortably warm; but in wet weather it was usually said that wearing them was only a decent way of going barefooted, and such, indeed, was the fact, owing to the spongy texture of the leather of which they were made.

Owing to the defective covering of the feet more than to anything else, the greater number of hunters and warriors were afflicted with rheumatism in the limbs. Of this disease they were all apprehensive in cold or wet weather, and therefore always slept with their feet to the fire, to prevent or cure it as well as they could. This kept them from being confirmed cripples for life.

In the latter years of the Indian war, our young men became more enamored of the Indian dress. The drawers were laid aside, and the leggins made longer, so as to reach the upper part of the thigh. The Indian breech-cloth was adopted. This was a piece of linen cloth, nearly a yard long and eight or nine inches broad, hanging before and behind over the belt, sometimes ornamented with coarse embroidery. To the same belt which secured the breech-cloth, strings, supporting the leggins, were attached. When this belt, as was often the case, passed over the hunting shirt, the upper part of the thighs and part of the hips were naked. The young warrior, instead of being abashed by his nudity, was proud of his Indian dress. In some few instances I have seen them go into places of public worship in this dress. Their appearance, however, did not much add to the devotion of the young ladies. The linsey coats and bed gowns, which were the universal dress of our women in early times, would make a strange figure at this day. They knew nothing of the ruffles, leghorns, curls, combs, rings, and other jewels with which the ladies now decorate themselves. Such things were not then to be had. Instead of the toilet, they had to hand the distaff or shuttle—the sickle or weeding hoe—contented if they could obtain their linsey clothing and cover their heads with a sunbonnet made of six or seven hundred linen.[14]

Schools

Our knowledge of eighteenth century schools in Franklin County is unfortunately limited. We know that there were such: Enoch Brown's was one of them. Moreover, the Scotch-Irish were a literate folk who read their Bibles and later attained an excellent reputation for learning. Perhaps this description, though it has a mildly sadistic tone, will convey an idea of an early school in our community.

Along the walls heavy planks rested on slanting pins and gave desk room for the older scholars who faced the wall when writing or cyphering, but faced the center of the room when not so engaged. Inside of this outer row of desks was a second row of low, backless slab benches, intended for the junior

128

members of the school. On these the smaller children had to sit all day with their feet dangling between the bench and the floor; nodding and trying to keep their balance on these slabs with out any back to lean against. This arrangement gave the master an open door when he wished to flog an offender without the formality of calling him up to the desk. It also left the unruly boy open to an attack from the rear, a disadvantage not to be neglected by the boy.

At one end of the room facing the school stood a table and chair—the throne of his majesty, the master. In front of the master's desk was a large open space, the flogging ground. The walls were devoid of all ornament—no maps, no charts, no pictures, no blackboards, no globes, no piano, no telephone—not one of the many things now deemed necessary for the equipment of a school. But instead of these were many articles of furniture not now in extensive use. First, a bundle of hickory or birch rods whose broken and splintered ends showed all too plainly that they were there for use, not for ornament. Second a furule or ruler, whose use may be explained later. Third, a "cat", a kind of scourge having a handle eighteen inches long, with nine narrow straps of sole leather of equal length nailed around one end. Think of the embryo sovereigns of this mighty Republic submitting to such punishment. The "strap" was also in evidence and was made of a strip of sole leather three-fourths of a yard long and three inches wide, doubled and stitched in the middle leaving two loops, one to pass the hand through, the other to strike. Besides these terrors was the dunce block on which an incorrigible lad was made to stand with no room to move a foot, book in hand, a pair of great wooden goggles on his nose, and on his head a high conical pasteboard cap having a cow's tail neatly appended behind, while in the front in great staring letters was the word "dunce" . . .

The New Testament was used as a text book in reading well down to the middle of the present century, and more than that, pupils were encouraged to commit to memory large portions of the Gospels for recitation on Saturday afternoon. Reading aloud had not become a lost art and pupils were taught to read with the spirit and the understanding, and "to mind their stops." Spelling, as well as reading, was taught in classes and the rivalry not only in individual schools, but among the various schools of a neighborhood was very keen. To be trapped in the home school, or to be spelled down in a match with another school was felt to be little short of a disgrace. The social events of the season were the spelling bees, which were held once a month in the evening and attended by old and young of the neighborhood.[15]

The same author tells us that a certain Thomas Kirby was among the first schoolmasters in Franklin County. He had a school at Back Creek in 1780 and opened the first grammar school in Chambersburg at the corner of Washington and Water Streets in 1790. Four years later he bought property on East Queen Street and brought James Ross in as his associate. When the new Chambersburg Academy was opened in 1797, Ross became the first headmaster and Kirby gave up schoolteaching and became a surveyor. James Ross was well versed in Latin and Greek and was wont to refer to Chambersburg as "Thalamapolis".[16] But this is many years later.

We have already spoken of the importance of mills of various sorts to the economy of the Valley. Indeed, the mill and the farm were the very first of our "industries". In this decade of peace mills multiplied rapidly on the Conococheague, the Falling Spring, the Conodoguinet, Herron's Branch, Rocky Spring, and Middle Spring. One writer says, "On three streams I have located more than one hundred different manufactories run by water".[17] In addition to grist mills and saw mills there were water-powered fulling, oil, clover, flax, hemp, sumac, sickle, and rolling mills.

One might think that with the coming of peace the traditional frontier house of logs—certainly in the established villages such as Chambersburg—would give way to more permanent structures of stone or brick. This appears not to have happened until much later. We are told that in 1785, for instance, there were only three stone buildings in Chambersburg: Chambers's Fort, John Jack's Tavern, and Nicholas Snider's smithy. The remainder were built of logs; there were none of brick.[18]

CHAPTER V.   THE REVOLUTIONARY YEARS

For more than a dozen years before the outbreak of hostilities between Great Britain and her American colonies, forces were building up that would inevitably lead to an explosion. Behind most of the unfortunate events of these years lay a policy known as mercantilism. The colonies were rich storehouses of raw materials which British merchants desired to transport to the mother country for their own profit. But the landed gentry in England were not sure whether the colonies were of financial benefit or not.

The colonies had always been of special importance to the merchants; but country gentlemen had grudgingly accepted the mercantilist proposition that the landed interests were dependent upon commerce. Mercantilists taught that the colonies gave business not only to merchants and manufacturers, to shipbuilders and seamen, but also indirectly to the British "husbandman who raises provisions to feed all these useful people".[20] In 1764, however, the country gentry were more impressed by the costs of the colonies than by the profits to be derived from them. British taxpayers were groaning under burdens left by the Seven Years' War, waged, supposedly, in the interests of the colonies; and they resented additions to the normal charges of maintaining the American plantations. The British government had long been accustomed to encourage certain colonial industries by granting bounties on products imported into England. The British exchequer shared the expenses of civil government and of provincial military forces in the younger colonies, while forces of the establishment had been stationed in America even before the French and Indian War. The colonial customs system, strangely enough, cost more than it brought in, until after its reorganization in 1768. Englishmen who had no special interest in America quite naturally begrudged to the Americans naval stations and fleets, supplies for the army, parliamentary grants to the colonies that had given special service in the war, presents for the red men exchanged for promises of peace, and all the other charges upon the British exchequer. In particular, the country gentlemen rebelled against the new expenses in America after 1763, for they objected to the terms of the peace, and wondered why Great Britain had taken Canada instead of rich islands in the West Indies. The merchants looked forward to expanding markets for British manufactures, but the country gentlemen were intent upon their present distresses.[1]

The same author describes the mercantilist's position toward the colonies even more explicitly in the following paragraph:

Before the middle of the eighteenth century men valued colonies almost exclusively for the commercial advantages to be derived from them. The following is a typical mercantilist explanation of the value of colonial possessions. "Great Britain and Ireland (for I wish to consider them as united in interest and connection with the colonies) stand in pretty much the same relation to the colonies as a manufacturing farmer's house and garden in the village, does to his adjacent farm." The

Benjamin Chambers

mercantilist went on to explain that the garden was sufficient to supply the farmer and his family with many necessaries and delicacies, while he could bring from his farm materials for manufacturing and bulky materials for market. It would make no difference to whom he sold the materials he did not need. "His chief care is that his own teams are the carriers, that the money his products are sold for is brought back to him, and that his servants do not lay out their wages at other shops than his."[2]

According to this view the American colonies were possessions to be exploited for the benefit of the mother country, her trade, and her wealth. The people of the colonies were not openly called serfs or even second-class citizens, but it gradually became apparent to them that, in the minds of many across the Atlantic, they were considered the tools of the mercantile interests. And when the powerful forces of mercantilism were supported after 1760 by a King who wished—contrary to British tradition in the eighteenth century—to rule by the royal will, it was inevitable that trouble of large proportion lay ahead.

Not that no contrary voices were raised in Britain in the next years. There were many. Edmund Burke, the most brilliant Irishman of his generation, was a staunch supporter of the colonists' position and a sharp critic of the unyielding policies of the government. As we read his "Speech on American Taxation" (19 April 1774) and the clear and cogent "Speech on Conciliation with America" (22 March 1775), we marvel that his logic and good will did not prevail; but these stormy years were marked by neither logic nor good will.

Mercantilist economic policy is not alone enough to explain British conduct toward the American colonies in these years. As shown in the first quotation above, the colonies were something of a financial burden to the mother country. King George believed that they should contribute financially toward their protection and toward the costs of administration. With this view it is hard to quarrel. One must seriously question, however, the prudence of certain of the measures taken to secure the desired financial contributions.

Examples of imprudent measures jump to mind. In 1764, the government imposed a tax on imports by the colonies and in the same year strengthened the Molasses Act which gave a monopoly to West Indian sugar growers. In the next year came the Stamp Act, which required that a stamp be affixed to a variety of documents. If the writers of the act had been more astute, they would not have included newspapers among these documents; for at once the press raised a clamor and whipped up public opinion with the now familiar outcry, "Taxation without representation".

But before the Stamp Act was finally passed in London, advance warning had been received by the colonies. So great was the feeling against it that on 5 October 1764 representatives of the colonies met in New York in the so-called "Stamp Act Congress" to discuss this Act and the Molasses Act. One of the chief abuses of the Stamp Act, from the point of view of colonial merchants, was that the tax had to be paid in bullion, thus weakening the colonies' balance of trade; for bullion was very scarce. British merchants also fought this tax as obstructing the collection of commercial debts. So great was the outcry that the Act was soon repealed.

As if learning nothing from this experience, the government in 1767 imposed a tax on American imports of paper, glass, lead, and tea. There was rage in the colonies. John Dickinson wrote his celebrated *Letters from a Farmer* in which he denied the authority of Parliament to tax without the consent of the taxed but showed no disloyalty to the King. The colonial assemblies made a non-importation agreement among themselves and established a boycott so successful that imports from Britain fell sharply. This led to the removal of all duties except the duty on tea.

Thus the stage was set for the Boston Tea Party of December 1773. Parliament, on the initiative of Lord North, had granted the East India Company the right to ship tea direct to the colonies without an import duty. This not only gave the East India Company a virtual monopoly of the tea trade but it was also so plainly discriminatory in favor of this somewhat shady mercantile venture that colonial feeling boiled over. Every child knows that a band of men dressed as Indians tossed the bales of tea into Boston Harbor. We cannot help thinking of James Smith and his Black Boys who, in 1765, dressed as Indians and burned the supplies destined for the Indians of the west. Both actions were illegal, but the motives were quite different. Smith's motive was to prevent military supplies from reaching hostile hands. The men who staged the Tea Party were out for revenge.

This act was scathingly denounced in and out of Parliament as the wanton destruction of private property by lawless and irresponsible thugs. Many cheered the incident in the colonies, but in London this abrupt action hardened conservative opinion against the colonials. Thus in April of the next year Parliament passed the Regulating Act, often referred to as the Coercion Acts. The Massachusetts Assembly was suspended; this colony was declared to be under Crown rule, *i.e.*, military rule; the port of Boston was closed, all judges in Massachusetts were to be appointed by the Crown; and throughout all the colonies troops were to be quartered in order to preserve the peace.

The decisive incident which in the retrospect appears to have made the Revolution inevitable, as it actually brought it upon the scene, was the Regulating Act of April, 1774, which annulled the charter of Massachusetts, and left that commonwealth to be ruled by a military governor. This atrocious measure, which was emphatically condemned by the most enlightened public sentiment in England, was the measure of a half-crazy young king, carried through a parliament in which more than a hundred members sat for rotten boroughs. It was the first violent manifestation of despotic tendency at the seat of government since 1688; and in this connection it is interesting to remember that in 1684 Charles II had undertaken to deal with Massachusetts precisely as was attempted ninety years later by George III. In both cases the charter was annulled, and a military governor appointed; and in both cases the liberties of all the colonies were openly threatened by the tyrannical scheme. But in the earlier case the conduct of James II at once brought on acute irritation in England, so that the evil was promptly removed. In the later case the evil was realized so much sooner and so much more acutely in the colonies than in England as to result in political separation.[3]*

Now indeed the fat was in the fire. Loud voices

*Appendix H

138

everywhere throughout the colonies shouted "tyranny", "despotism", liberty!", "freedom!". Within a month of the passage of the Coercion Acts Paul Revere was in Philadelphia to win the support of Pennsylvania. In September a Congress was held in Philadelphia at which the members agreed to cease all trade with Britain until the Coercion Acts should be rescinded and drafted a petition respectfully asking Parliament to rescind also thirteen commercial acts passed since 1763. The petition was rejected with contempt.

But the people of Cumberland County anticipated most of these Congressional actions by two months. On 12 July 1774 the freemen of the county met at Carlisle, debated at length, and drew up a series of resolutions condemning Parliament for closing the port of Boston; recommending a General Congress of colonies—which, as we have seen, was held in September; and calling for a boycott of British merchandise. Some students of our local history have expressed surprise that these actions were taken so soon and so far away from the seat of the trouble. The temper of the meeting is best seen in the first resolution:

> *Resolved.* That the late act of the parliament of Great Britain, by which the port of Boston is shut up, is oppressive to that town, and subversive of the rights and liberties of the Colony of Massachusetts Bay; that the principle upon which that act is founded, is not more subversive of the rights and liberties of that colony, than it is of all other British colonies in North America; and, therefore, the inhabitants of Boston are suffering in the common cause of all these colonies.[4]

One wonders indeed at this immediate and generous response. These people of the Cumberland Valley had had their war, nine cruel years of it, and had been devastated by it from 1755 onward. No other province had come to their help: not any New England province, not New York, not New Jersey, not Delaware. Maryland was still cool because of the perennial border dispute. Virginia had the same troubles and could send no aid. The Carolinas were too remote to help. So the men of the Cumberland Valley assumed the full burden of their war. Not even the government in Philadelphia really helped, with the exception of the Provincial forts and the expedition of 1756 against Kittanning, sponsored by the government but carried out without exception by men from the Valley. Not until the government sent Col. Bouquet against Pontiac did the Valley receive substantial assistance against the French and Indian menace; and the aim of the government was chiefly to secure the western borders, not to protect the battered people of the Valley frontier.

Surely some new ferment was at work now. The people of the Valley set aside any ill feeling they may have harbored against the people of New England and offered their unstinting help, both in principle and in practice, to the colonists of Massachusetts. A new and uniting spirit was here. It was the acceptance of what the Cumberland County resolution called a "common cause" that carried the provincials through the hardships and discouragements of the next eight years.

Events now began to move with inevitable and fateful speed. The military governor of Massachusetts, General Thomas Gage, tried to enforce martial law, but he had only 4,000 troops whereas the patriots had nearly

10,000, drilling, watching, waiting. The colonials were buying arms from France, Spain, and the Netherlands, importing them in containers labelled "spirits" and storing them at Concord.

On 18 April came Paul Revere's famous ride and on the next day the Battle of Lexington. Seventeen days later, on 5 May, a meeting was held at Carlisle. This description of it occurs in a letter written the next day:

> Yesterday the County committee met from nineteen townships, on the short notice they had. Above three thousand men have already associated, the arms returned amounted to about fifteen hundred. The committee have voted five hundred effective men, besides commissioned officers, to be immediately drafted, taken into pay, armed and disciplined, to march on the first emergency, to be paid and supported as long as necessary, by a tax on all estates, real and personal in the county.[5]

A day later the same committee voted to recruit 1,500 or 2,000 men if needed, and to put the county in debt by as much as £27,000 if necessary.

This was not mere talk. Men were enlisted, officers appointed, arms and other military supplies were assembled.

> One morning in Carlisle in July, 1775, a drumbeat was heard in the streets that roused the citizens from their beds to learn the meaning of the unwonted sound. In a few minutes the news was carried from house to house that the unusual stir was occasioned by the arrival of the company of riflemen under Capt. James Chambers from Conococheague, on the way to Cambridge, to assist in the leaguer of

141

Boston. The company marched by way of Harris'
Ferry, Bethlehem, and New Windsor, on the
Hudson above West Point, and arrived at
Cambridge on the 7th of August. The men wore
white frocks, or hunting shirts, and round hats. They
were expert with the rifle, and often picked off
British officers and soldiers at double the distance of
common musket shot.

At Cambridge the Pennsylvania companies
were formed into battalion under Col. William
Thompson. This organization was known as
"Colonel Thompson's Battalion of Riflemen". The
riflemen were placed on the outposts of the
American lines near Prospect Hill. The men from
Conococheague were on the ground scarcely
twenty-four hours before they exchanged shots with
the enemy, and on the 26th day of August, Captain
Chambers was in command of a detachment that in
a spirited action prevented the occupation of
Ploughed Hill. Two days later his only son,
Benjamin, a lad scarcely twelve years old, was with
him on Ploughed Hill, when the enemy made a
demonstration as if intending to storm the works.
The company, with the rest of the command,
remained on the American front, facing Bunker Hill
until early in April, 1776, when the regiment was
sent to New Utrecht, on Long Island.[6]

Thus from what is now Franklin County, led by a captain
from Chambersburg, came the first body of soldiers from
south and west of the Hudson River to go to the aid of
Boston. They, with others from Maryland, made a profound impression on the New Englanders.

Several companies of riflemen, amounting, it is said, to more than fourteen hundred men, have arrived here from Pennsylvania and Maryland, a distance of from five hundred to seven hundred miles. They are remarkably stout and hardy men, many of them exceeding six feet in height. They are dressed in white frocks or rifle shirts, and round hats. These men are remarkable for the accuracy of their aim, striking a mark with great certainty at two hundred yards distance. At a review a company of them, while on a quick advance, fired their balls into objects of seven inches diameter, at a distance of two hundred and fifty yards. They are now stationed on our out lines, and their shot have frequently proved fatal to British officers and soldiers who exposed themselves to view, even at more than double the distance of a common musket shot.[7]*

The Battle of Breed's Hill and Bunker Hill had occurred on 17 June before Captain James Chambers and his men arrived. Everyone was watchful and tense; and we feel this mood as we read a letter from Captain James to his wife in Chambersburg.

> Cambridge, August 13, 1775.
> My Dear Kitty: We arrived in camp on the 7th ult., about 12 o'clock. We were not here above an hour until we went to view the lines where the English camp is all in plain sight. We crossed the lines, and went beyond the outposts to a small hill, within musket-shot of a man-of-war and and a floating battery, and not further from the works at the foot of Bunker Hill, where we could see them very plainly. Whilst I was standing there, some of our

*Appendix I

riflemen slipped down——Hill, about a gunshot to the left of us, and began firing. The Regulars returned it without hurting our men. We thought we saw one of the red coats fall. Since the riflemen came here, by the latest accounts from Boston, there have been forty-two killed, and thirty-eight prisoners taken at the Lighthouse, twelve of the latter Tories. Amongst the killed are four captains, one of them the son of a Lord, and worth £40,000 a year, whose name I cannot recollect. The riflemen go where they please, and keep the Regulars in continual hot water.

They are every day firing cannon at our people, but have not yet killed a man. We expect six wagons loaded with powder here in two or three days; and when they arrive, our twenty-four pounders will begin to play on their ships and the lines on Bunker Hill. It is difficult for our men to get within shot of them, as they have floating batteries that flank the end of Winter hill, and men-of-war on the other side, though our boys think they killed several of them about an hour ago. I saw a small cannonading between two of the enemy's boats and one of our batteries to the north of Boston. We can see all the town distinctly from our fort on Prospect Hill, and it is a very pretty place. . . . . Two deserters came to us last night.[8]

The last two sentences of a letter written about a fortnight later must have been read by Kitty with mixed emotions:

Camp at Cambridge, Aug. 29, 1776

My Dear Kitty:

144

. . . . On the evening of the 26th inst., Saturday, I was ordered to draw fifty men out of each of the Cumberland companies, and be ready to march at sunset. Accordingly I did so, and marched without beat of drum to Prospect Hill, and thence proceeded with the riflemen stationed there—in all about four hundred;—to Ploughed Hill and then down the hill within three or four hundred yards of the enemy's strongest works, to cover a party of about two thousand musketmen, who were at the same time to entrench on Ploughed Hill.

They labored very hard all night, and at daybreak had the redoubt nearly completed. When the English discovered our defences so near, they began a heavy cannonading which continued all day. They killed with their cannon balls one adjutant and one soldier, and wounded three others with musket balls. These were close to the floating batteries and their field works. Mr. William Simpson of Paxton, a volunteer, was struck by a shot and his foot carried away.

On Monday we were with about fifteen thousand men on Ploughed Hill, as the enemy made every appearance of coming out to storm our works, but thought it not good for their health, and so returned to Boston. They fired several cannon from Bunker Hill, and killed one man on Ploughed Hill. This last point is about six hundred yards from Bunker's, where is their strongest force. Your son Benjamin sends his love to you. He was with me in all this affair.[9]

We must now take our leave of Captain James for a time and follow events in Philadelphia. In November the

Assembly of Pennsylvania met to appoint delegates to represent the province in the Congress soon to be held. Against the background of the warlike events in and near Boston, it is surprising to discover how moderate and yet firm were the instructions they gave to their delegates:

> . . . that they, in behalf of this colony, dissent from, and utterly reject any proposition, should such be made, that may cause or lead to a separation from our mother country, or a change of the form of government.[10]

This was the mood of the Assembly seven months after Lexington and eight months before the framing of the Declaration of Independence.

But this was not the mood of Congress. In January of 1776 Congress issued a call for more troops, and the Cumberland Valley responded by raising four new battalions, consisting of eight companies, of which three were mostly from Franklin County.[11] Not content with the moderate stand of the Pennsylvania Assembly, Congress recommended its abolition on 10 May. Cowed by this threat and possibly influenced by a patriotic petition forwarded by the freemen of Cumberland County on 28 May, the Assembly revoked its instructions on 14 June, stating that "we now think ourselves justifiable in removing the restrictions laid upon you by those instructions."[12]

It is well to review these events if only to point out again the well known fact that the colonies were not yet ready to break the bond with the mother country and the further fact that many of the colonists were Tories, still deeply loyal to the Crown. On the floor of Congress there was a long and often bitter dispute over the question of independence. When Richard Henry Lee of Virginia offered his resolution calling for independence on 7 June, seven provinces favored it and six, including Pennsylvania, did not. But by the end of June opinion had hardened and only New York held out; and when the final vote came it was unanimous except that the delegates from New York abstained, saying they had no instructions.

The days of the Pennsylvania Assembly were numbered. The spirit of the times was against it if only, because it represented the *ancien régime*. It had lost the confidence of Congress, as we have seen; it equally lost the confidence of the population at large. On 19 July 1776 a Constitutional Convention met in Philadelphia and ratified a new constitution for Pennsylvania on 28 September, this new instrument to take effect in November. Cumberland County sent eight delegates to this Convention, one of whom, James McLene, came from Franklin County. The death of the old Assembly was also the death knell of the Proprietors and of the Quaker political influence.

Fired by these events, and now by the news that General Howe had just received a great reinforcement of troops, bringing his army to nearly 25,000 men, the men of the Cumberland Valley flocked to the colors. By 16 August thirteen companies, fully equipped, had left to join Washington's army. Four were from Franklin County, led by James McConnell, William Huston, Robert Culbertson, and Conrad Schneider.[13]

Most militant of all were certain of the clergymen of the Valley—members indeed of the Church Militant. We remember the Rev. John Steele, his fort at Church Hill, and his preaching with his gun at hand during the Indian troubles. Mr. Steele was now pastor of a church at Carlisle; and though beyond the age of military service, he exhorted his congregation to go and fight for the liberty of the nation. This was true also of the Rev. Robert Cooper, A.M., D.D., pastor of the Middle Spring Presbyterian Church. In August of 1775 he preached a stirring sermon entitled "Courage in a Good Cause" which was printed and widely circulated. Acting on his own words, he became a chaplain in Washington's forces and fought side by side with his men at the Battle of Trenton.[14]

Another ardent patriot was the Rev. John King, who addressed a newly formed company from Montgomery, Peters, and Hamilton townships in these words:

> The case is plain; life must be hazarded or all is gone. You must go and fight, or send your humble submission, and bow as a beast to its burden, or as an ox to the slaughter. The King of Great Britain has declared us rebels, a capital crime; submission therefore consents to the rope or the ax. Liberty is doubtless gone; none could imagine a tyrant king should be more favorable to conquered rebels, than he was to loyal, humble and petitioning subjects. No! No! If ever a people lay in chains we must, if our enemies carry their point against us, and oblige us to unconditional submission. This is not all. Our Tory neighbors will be our proud and tormenting enemies.[15]

But most celebrated of all our fiery clergy was the Rev. John Craighead, pastor of the church at Rocky Spring. His tale has been told many times by many persons, but we shall hear it from the pen of one who tells it with some of the poetic and religious fervor that must have marked Mr. Craighead's own words:

It was in the old log church that its first pastor, the Rev. Mr. Craighead, preached for many years . . . It is related that, upon one occasion, from the pulpit, the patriotic preacher declaimed in such burning and powerful terms against the wrongs we then were suffering, that after one glowing description of the duty of the men, the whole congregation rose from their seats, and declared their willingness to march to the conflict.

There was but one, tradition says, in the entire assembly, who was not overcome by the stirring appeal that was made, and that was an aged female, in whom maternal affection, recently caused to bleed, completely mastered both a sense of propriety and the love of liberty. "Stop, Mr. Craighead," she exclaimed; "I jist want to tell ye, agin you loss such a purty boy as I have, in the war, ye will na be so keen for fighting; quit talking, and gang yersel to the war. Yer always preaching to the boys about it, but I dinna think ye'd be very likely to gang yersel. Jist go and try it."

As we walk reverentially over the hill, we feel as if we were treading upon sacred ground—dedicated to God and American Liberty. We can almost fancy we see the man of God standing where we now stand, telling to the assembled multitude the story of their country's wrongs, and urging them to hesitate no longer which to choose, cowardly inactivity or the noble part of brave defenders of their country's rights. We hear him call on them as he stands before his old church, and requests those who desire to march with him to battle, to hesitate no longer, but place themselves by his side, and acknowledge him their commander, who will lead them to the field of battle, where they will save America, or perish in the cause of Freedom. One by one they approach their pastor, and soon a long line of dauntless spirits stretches across the green to the neighbouring wood . . . . .

At length the line is completed, and they are dismissed, to meet on the following Monday. Soon after the dawn of day, might be seen the sturdy husbandman, with gray hairs scattered over his brow, and the youth of few years, reaching down their old fire-arms, hither-to used only for beasts of prey, or the wild game, but now to be used for other purposes. They fling around their necks their rude powder-horns and bullet-pouches, and shouldering their guns, march to the place of rendezvous. As the eye wanders over the neighbourhood, in the distance they may be seen, one by one, drawing near the hill. Soon they are all assembled, and their company is organized, and after an eloquent appeal to the Almighty, the Reverend Captain places himself at their head, and the noble band marches off to battle. . . . The company joined the army of Washington, and gave undoubted evidence that their courage was of no mean order, but was based upon the hallowed principles of Christianity; which, although discountenancing bloodshed and war, does not forbid the oppressed to make an effort to throw off the yoke of the oppressor.

Their Captain engaged vigorously in the war, and during the hours spent in camp, habitually acted as chaplain to the soldiers. After the war was over, he returned to his charge, and faithfully watched over the congregation until the period of his death, which occurred in 1799.[16]

Despite these shows of patriotism on the home front—and they were matched by similar demonstrations in scores of communities—the American cause suffered a considerable setback in late August. Washington had hoped to make a *grand coup* on Long Island but suddenly reinforcements arrived for the enemy and Washington was forced to retreat. James Chambers, now promoted to the rank of lieutenant colonel, participated in this operation and left this account of it:

In Camp at Delamere's Mills, three miles above King's Bridge.

September 3, 1776

My Dear Kitty: I should have written to you sooner, but the hurry and confusion we have been in for some time past, has hindered me. I will now give you a short account of transactions in this quarter.

On the morning of the 22nd August there were nine thousand British troops on New Utrecht plains. The guard alarmed our small camp, and we assembled at the flagstaff. We marched our forces, about two hundred in number, to New Utrecht to watch the movements of the enemy. When we came on the hill, we discovered a party of them advancing toward us. We prepared to give them a warm reception, when an imprudent fellow fired, and they immediately halted and turned toward Flatbush. The main body also, moved along the great road toward the same place. We proceeded alongside of them in the edge of the woods as far as the turn of the lane, where the cherry-trees were, if you remember. We then found it impracticable for so small a force to attack them on the plain, and sent Captain Hamilton with twenty men, before them to burn all the grain; which he did very cleverly, and killed a great many cattle . . . .

Some of our men fired upon and killed several Hessians, as we ascertained two days afterwards. Strong guards were maintained all day on the flanks of the enemy, and our regiment and the Hessian yagers kept up a severe firing, with a loss of but two wounded on our side. We laid a few Hessians low, and made them retreat out of Flatbush. Our people went into the town, and brought the goods out of the burning houses.

The enemy liked to have lost their field-pieces. Captain Steel, of your vicinity, acted bravely. We would certainly have had the cannon had it not been for some foolish person calling retreat. The main body of the foe returned to the town; and when our lads came back, they told of their exploits. This was doubted by some, which enraged our men so much that a few of them ran and brought away several Hessians on their backs. This kind of firing by our riflemen and theirs continued until ten (two?) o'clock in the morning of the 26th, when our regiment was relieved by a portion of the Flying Camp; and we started for Fort Greene to get refreshment, not having lain down the whole of this time, and almost dead with fatigue. . . .

It was thought advisable to retreat off Long Island; and on the night of the 30th, it was done with great secrecy. Very few of the officers knew it until they were on the boats, supposing that an attack was intended. A discovery of our intention to the enemy would have been fatal to us. The Pennsylvania troops were done great honor by being chosen the *corps de reserve* to cover the retreat. The regiments of Colonels Hand, Hagan, Shea, and Hazlett were detailed for that purpose. We kept up fires, with outposts stationed, until all the rest were over. We left the lines after it was fair day, and then came off.

Never was a greater feat of generalship shown than in this retreat; to bring off an army of twelve thousand men within sight of a strong enemy, possessed of as strong a fleet as ever floated on our seas, without any loss, and saving all the baggage.

General Washington saw the last over himself.[17]

For his meritorious conduct throughout this ticklish retreat James Chambers was promoted to the rank of Colonel. His new commission bore the date 28 September 1776. "He was assigned to the command of the Tenth Regiment, Pennsylvania Line, March 12, 1777, but exactly a month later he was transferred to the First Pennsylvania, his old regiment, with which he remained until his retirement, January 17, 1781".[18]

The same author continues:

Colonel Chambers was in most of the battles of the campaigns of 1776-78. In the battle of the White Plains he had little part, as the action was not general. He was in the winter campaign of 1776-77, in New Jersey, but apparently was not in the battles of Trenton and Princeton. Our first positive knowledge of his whereabouts in the spring of 1777, was his presence in the Jerseys while Washington's meagre army was skirmishing with Lord Cornwallis.

He was one of the first officers to enter Brunswick, in June, when Cornwallis was forced to quit that place. His regiment was afterward encamped on the mountain back of the Bound Brook. On the 11th of August he reports his men "as all well and in high spirits, although much fatigued with constant and Long Marches." The regiment had marched from Mount Prospect, as the camp at Bound Brook was called, to Morristown; then to Pompton, from Pompton to the mouth of the Clove, and finally through the Clove to New Windsor. The army was watching Sir William Howe, whose devious movements were very puzzling. From New Windsor there was a countermarch—first across the Bridge to Chester, and then to Howell's ferry on the Delaware—by two divisions, of one of which the First Pennsylvania was a part; the main body of the army went by way of Morristown to Coryell's. After many days the weary soldiers reached the Falls of Schuylkill, above Philadelphia; on the 9th of August another countermarch was begun toward Coryell's, which brought Chambers to the camp at "Cross Roads," about twenty miles from Philadelphia, where his letter of the 11th was written.

At last Howe's mysterious expedition was reported at the Head of Elk. Washington, with his army, hastened through Philadelphia and met the enemy at the Brandywine. In the battle that ensued Colonel Chambers was conspicuous for his energy and courage. His regiment was engaged at very close range and suffered severely. Great exertion was required to save a howitzer that the artillerymen, when ordered to retreat, had abandoned. Although the enemy had come within thirty yards and his fire was very galling, Chambers succeeded in saving all the brigade artillery and retreated in good order to the next hill, where he was not followed. He received a Hessian bullet in his side, of which he made light in his letters, but which gave him much trouble during the rest of his life.[19]

Col. James Chambers has left his own vivid account of this engagement, again in a letter. Brandywine was undoubtedly the most hazardous incident in which he was implicated during the war.

> My Dear—
>
> . . . . On the morning of the 11th Sept., 1777, we were apprised that the enemy was advancing; and soon after heard the engagement between our light troops and their advanced parties. Whilst their main design was in front to our right, the cannon ceased firing except now and then; and small detachments of our troops were constantly skirmishing with them. But in a short while, we found that they had crossed the Brandywine near the forks, and were coming in flank of our right wing. The cannonade commenced about three o'clock, but soon gave way to small arms, which continued like an incessant clap of thunder till within an hour of sunset, when our people filed off. Then the attack began with us on the left. But I must observe to you that while the right was engaged, the troops that were on the right of our brigade on the hill were drawn off . . . . and left our right flank quite uncovered. The enemy kept an unremitted fire from their

artillery (and ours too, played with great fury) until advancing under the thick smoke they took possession of the redoubt in front of our park.

As there were no troops to cover the artillery in the redoubt—the enemy was within thirty yards before being discovered—our men were forced to fly and to leave three pieces behind. Our brigade was drawn into line, with the park of artillery two hundred yards in the rear of the redoubt. Our park was ordered off then, and my right exposed. The enemy advanced on the hill where our park was, and came within fifty yards of the hill above me. I then ordered my men to fire. Two or three rounds made the lads clear the ground.

The General sent orders for our artillery to retreat—it was on my right—and ordered me to cover it with—of my regiment. It was done, but to my surprise the artillerymen had run and left the howitzer behind. The two field pieces went up the road protected by about sixty of my men, who had very warm work, but brought them safe. I then ordered another party to fly to the howitzer and bring it off. Captain Buchanan, Lieutenant Stimson, and Lieutenant Douglass went immediately to the gun, and the men followed their example, and I covered them with the few I had remaining. But before this could be done, the main body of the foe came within thirty yards, and kept up the most terrible fire I suppose ever heard in America; though with very little loss on our side. I brought all the brigade artillery safely off, and I hope to see them again fired at the scoundrels. Yet we retreated to the next height in good order, in the midst of a very

156

heavy fire of cannon and small arms. Not thirty yards distant, we formed to receive them, but they did not choose to follow.

I lost Lieutenants Halliday and Wise killed; Captain Grier was badly wounded, Captain Craig and myself slightly wounded. I have, I suppose, lost six or seven killed, and about the same number wounded. We lost several fine officers out of the brigade.[20]*

The Battle of Brandywine was another setback for the patriots. Washington was compelled to retreat and General Howe marched triumphantly into Philadelphia, where he and his officers spent a winter wining and dining while Washington and his ill-clad and hungry soldiers suffered at Valley Forge. Early in 1778 Howe resigned as Commander of the British forces in America and Sir Henry Clinton replaced him. When in April the news reached Clinton that twelve French ships-of-the-line had sailed from Toulon for New York carrying 4,000 soldiers, he abandoned Philadelphia in order to protect New York. As he crossed New Jersey with about 10,000 troops, Washington's army followed and there was a sharp engagement at Monmouth Court House. Here is Col. James's account:

The attack commenced at eleven o'clock, and a most violent cannonade continued for nearly five hours; in which time both armies were manoeuvring on the right and left. Our Division was drawn in front of our artillery in a small hollow, while the enemy's artillery was placed on an eminence in front of our brigade. Of course, we were in a right line of their fire, both parties playing their cannon over our

*Appendix J

157

heads, and yet only killed two of our men, and wounded four of my regiment with splinters of rails. Our army out-generalled them, and at the same time advanced some baggage across a swamp, and drove them before us. They fled in all quarters, and at sunset we had driven them near to Monmouth town. We encamped on the field that night.

They left on the ground several officers of distinction, amongst them Colonel Monckton; and yesterday we buried upwards of two hundred and fifty of the bold Britons who were to conquer the world!

I rode over the whole ground, and saw two hundred of their dead. It is surprising that we lost not more than thirty. However, of this I can assure you, that for every ten of them I did not see one of ours killed. During yesterday, our fatigue parties were collecting the dead in piles, and burying them. The enemy is flying with precipitation to the Hook, and we are now on our march to Brunswick. They desert very fast, so watch for news.

J.C.

The British loss was about three hundred killed in battle; the American not seventy, while both armies suffered some mortality from fatigue and the excessive heat.[21]

Seilhamer now carries the story forward:

After Monmouth, when the army was again at White Plains, he was in command of the First Pennsylvania Brigade. During the long watch on the Hudson that followed he continued assiduously in the performance of his military duties. He dined with Washington on the 17th of August, as one of the officers of the day, and the orderly books shows that he was afterward a frequent guest at the Commander-in-Chief's table. His regiment was in the attack on the Bergen block-house, July 19, 1780. This was probably the last action in which it was engaged, while under his command.[22]

Another of Col. James's letters to Kitty describes the fray at Bergen block-house and concludes thus:

You may depend your son is a good soldier. All the officers and men say he behaved exceedingly well. I had not the pleasure of seeing it, as I lay very sick at the time. Ben can tell you plenty of news about fighting.[23]

When the Pennsylvania Line was reorganized on 17 January 1781, Col. James retired after five and a half years of continuous service. His bullet wound sustained at Brandywine still troubled him. He longed to be with Kitty again and with their children. Moreover, his father was now in his early seventies and needed him to help look after the family property. So he mustered out, taking young Ben with him and also the respect and affection of his fellow-officers and men.

More than one local historian has lamented the lack of colorful information about the men who left Franklin County to fight in the Revolutionary War. There are rosters of troops by regiment, battalion, and company— very helpful to anyone who wishes to trace an ancestor but in themselves only lifeless lists. They may be found, these lists, in the *History of Franklin County*, published in Chicago in 1887. They make dull reading. Other facts are to be found in the many genealogical tables of early settlers. One must ask, with regret and sadness, whether anything has less life and human rondure than a genealogy. Dates of birth, death, marriage, children; what are the people like whose vital statistics we read?

Yet we know something about James McCalmont, the intrepid and resourceful Indian-fighter of twenty years ago.

No mention of McCalmont is found from the end of the French and Indian War until the breaking out of the Revolutionary War when he hastened to enter the service of his Country, and on the same day the Declaration of Independence had been passed in Congress, (July 4, 1776) a military Convention, representing the fifty-three battalions of the Associators of Pennsylvania, met at Lancaster to choose two Brigadier Generals to command the battalions and forces of Pennsylvania. Cumberland County was represented by Col. John Armstrong, Lieutenant Colonels Wm. Blair, Wm. Clark, and Frederick Watts; Major, James McCalmont of Letterkenny township.

The sixth battalion was commanded by Col. Samuel Culbertson, who had been a Lieutenant Colonel in the first but was promoted to the command of the sixth. John Work was the Lieutenant Colonel and James McCalmont, Major. The battalion was composed of eight companies from Lurgan, Letterkenny, Hamilton, Peters and Montgomery townships and at least two of the battalions' officers and three or four of the captains were from the Rocky Spring Congregation.

In 1777 when the British occupied Philadelphia, McCalmont had command of a troop of

Rangers, whose business it was to prevent the Tories of the interior from furnishing provisions to their friends in the city.

In the early part of 1777, James Smith who was a member of the Assembly from Westmoreland County, obtained leave of absence and formed a company of forest adventurers and with this company went to the Army in New Jersey. They attacked about two hundred British at Rocky Hill, and with only thirty-six men drove them from their position. On another occasion they took twenty-two Hessians together with their officers, baggage, wagons and a number of continental prisoners they were guarding. In a few days, Col. Smith was taken ill with camp fever and returned home, and Major McCalmont was placed in command and did some daring feats:—It is said he was not only brave but an accomplished soldier. Upon one occasion on one of his raids in New Jersey, opposite Philadelphia, he captured about a dozen Hessian soldiers. Having no convenient way to dispose of them, he marched them to Strasburg and induced them to settle there; to one he gave a few acres of land, to another a tannery and to another a tavern stand and for the others he made provisions in manner suitable to their several capacities. According to "Men of Mark", the United States Barracks erected at Carlisle in 1777 were built by the Hessian soldiers captured on this occasion. Of the Hessians brought to Strasburg, a few of their descendants still remain and are among the respected citizens of that locality. They were, however, considered just a little different from other people.[24]

And we also know something about the fabled Molly Pitcher. She was not, for instance, Mary Hays Ludwig, to whose memory a handsome monument was erected at Carlisle in 1876. The true Molly Pitcher was Margaret Cochran Corbin, born of Covenanter parents who settled near Rocky Spring before 1750.

Of these patriots and pioneers of the past we must not forget the memory and deeds of Margaret Cochran, whose father was killed by the Indians in one of their murderous inroads in 1756. Margaret became the wife of John Corbin, and when he enlisted in Captain Francis Proctor's first company of Pennsylvania artillery, she accompanied him to the tented field. During the attack by the British on Fort Washington Corbin was killed and as there was no one to take his place the officer in command ordered the gun to be withdrawn. When the patriotic Margaret heard of it she volunteered to take the place of her dead husband and nobly did her duty, helping to load and fire the gun until severely wounded. The Supreme Council of Pennsylvania recognized her services with a pension and Congress unanimously resolved "that Margaret Corbin, wounded and disabled at the battle of Fort Washington while she heroically filled the post of her husband, who was killed by her side serving a piece of artillery, do receive during her natural life, on condition of said disability, one-half the monthly pay drawn by a soldier in the service of these states, and that she now receive, out of the public stores, one suit of clothes or value thereof in money".[25]

After the war Margaret Cochran Corbin went to live with

army friends at Swimtown (now Highland Falls), N.Y. and died there in 1800. Her body was brought to West Point in 1926 by the National Society Daughters of the American Revolution and a granite monument erected to her memory.

It is significant that we hear nothing of Tory activity in the Cumberland Valley in these war years. In the summer of 1777 patriots in Philadelphia tried to force loyalists into line and arrested about 40 prominent persons suspected of disloyalty to the new government. Only a few proved to be outright Tories. There was a small flurry of fear in the Valley the next spring when three long-suspected Tories at Fort Pitt deserted to the British and another small band was known to be active over the mountains in the Juniata Valley. The British were still comfortably in control of Philadelphia and Washington's army had not yet recovered from the winter at Valley Forge. So the Tories laid their plans to seize the land and property of patriots in the Juniata and Cumberland Valleys if the American cause foundered.[26] These men were believed to be arousing the Indians against patriotic whites. A recurrence of the old Indian troubles was a constant fear in the Cumberland Valley during the war years when so many of the men were absent.

On 12 April 1779 the Supreme Executive Council of Pennsylvania, moved by the strong anti-British feeling of the times and by obvious cupidity, issued a declaration of treason and forfeiture of property. Many 'traitors' lost their legal status and their property as a result of this act. No traitors were cited from Cumberland County. "Throughout this great Valley, a Tory, a name applied in Revolutionary times to a person opposed to the war and in favor of British claims, was rare, if to be found at all."[27]

When Cornwallis and his beleaguered army of 7,000 surrendered at Yorktown on 19 October 1781, there was consternation in Britain and mad rejoicing in the colonies. It was true that Washington had yet to deal with General Clinton, who held New York, but everyone knew the end had come and that the war was over.

In March of 1782 the ill-starred Lord North resigned and was followed by Rockingham, who formed a government on the basis of independence for the colonies. He died before he could effect his wishes, but his successor, Lord Shelburne, entered into peace negotiations with the now independent country, and on 30 November 1783 the Treaty of Paris was signed—the second Treaty of Paris to affect the fortunes of the colonies in less than 20 years. Congress ratified it in the following April. The eastern border with Canada was established; western lands as far as the Mississippi River were assigned to the United States; and the New England states received fishing rights off Newfoundland—an agreement of great importance to these maritime states.

Now that peace has been declared and the men who served in the Continental Army have returned to their homes, we may pause to read the reflections of some later commentators on these events. J. H. Stoner writes, "It is confidently believed that, in proportion to area and to population, no section [of Pennsylvania] furnished more officers and soldiers in the Revolutionary War than the Cumberland Valley.[28] George Chambers cites two generals and eight colonels from the Cumberland Valley "and majors, captains and subalterns in numbers too great to be enumerated here, whilst its soldiers in the rank and file were in numbers little below the taxables of their district."[29]

In a different and much broader perspective as he looks back over the war and its causes, Fiske writes:

> In the light of the foregoing narrative it distinctly appears that, while the American Revolution involved a military struggle between the governments of Great Britain and the United States, it did not imply any essential antagonism of interests or purposes between the British and American peoples. It was not a contest between Englishmen and Americans, but between two antagonistic principles of government, each of which had its advocates and opponents in both countries. It was a contest between Whig and Tory principles, and it was the temporary prevalence of Toryism in the British government that caused the political severance between the two countries. If the ideas of Walpole, or the ideas of Chatham, had continued to prevail at Westminster until the end of the eighteenth century, it is not likely that any such political severance would have occurred. The self-government of the American colonies would not have been interfered with, and such slight grievances as here and there existed might easily have been remedied by the ordinary methods of peace. The American Revolution, unlike most political revolutions, was essentially conservative in character. It was not caused by actually existing oppression, but by the determination to avoid possible oppression in future. Its object was not the acquisition of new liberties, but the preservation of old ones. The principles asserted in the Stamp Act Congress of 1765 differed in no essential respect from those that had been proclaimed five centuries earlier, in Earl

Simon's Parliament of 1265. Political liberty was not an invention of the western hemisphere; it was brought to these shores from Great Britain by our forefathers of the seventeenth century, and their children of the eighteenth naturally refused to surrender the treasure which from time immemorial they had enjoyed.[30]

A thought-provoking summary view of the war is offered by R. L. Smith in his book entitled *It All Happened Once Before:*

> In A.D. 1763 the French and Indian Wars came to a close on the Western Hemisphere; with the victory going to the British and their claims to the 13 colonies standing undisputed. But the cessation of hostilities on the American side was only a breathing spell preluding almost fifty years of desparate struggles in Europe, during which no major power dared risk any great engagement outside the continent. So hard pressed was England that, when the American colonies declared their independence and launched their war of liberty, it became necessary to hire German mercenaries to cross the Atlantic to fight Britain's battles for her. There was no time during the Revolutionary War when England was represented in America by more than a very few thousands of her troops, or more than a small fraction of her Navy. Again competent historians agree that those few years between 1763 and 1815 (the close of the Napoleonic Wars) represent the only period in at least 300 years during which the American republic could have established itself as a free nation.[31]

CHAPTER VI: GROWTH AND CONSOLIDATION

In the Cumberland Valley immigration and emigration had long been one of the facts of life.

> The old tax lists disclose that the movement from this valley to other sections began before the Revolution, assumed larger proportions after that time, and continued well into the next century.[1]

Encouraged now by the successful conclusion of the war and stirred as always by the lure of adventure, a new flow of emigration began.

> After the Revolution the flow of emigration westward became a wave. At the close of the eighteenth century, nearly every one of our early families had a footing in western Pennsylvania, Ohio, Indiana or Kentucky.[2]

Those who left were mostly the Scotch-Irish. They sold their lands easily and amicably to neighbors of German extraction; and thus the gradual transformation began which brought our German population into control of a large proportion of the farm lands of Franklin County. But despite constant emigration the population of Franklin County increased.

We have seen that Chambersburg was laid out by Col. Chambers in 1764. Eighteen years later Greencastle was laid out by John Allison. The first settler is said to have been John Smith, who conveyed the land to William Allison before 1751. When the later Allison decided to turn his land into a town, he had the help of an early schoolteacher, James Crawford, who had served in the recent war. These two laid out 256 lots which were sold in the usual way of those days, by lottery, for the equivalent of $8 each plus an annual quit-rent of ten shillings.[3] It is possible that Allison and Crawford knew that Franklin County would come into being two years hence, for we have seen how eagerly the new town of Greencastle sought to become the county seat.

The year 1783 saw not only the signing of the Treaty of Paris but also the birth of a new and lucrative industry in the Cumberland Valley. It was in that year that three Chambers brothers, William, Benjamin, and George, opened the first iron works—and later a forge—at Mount Pleasant, about three miles north of Fort Loudon. The deposits of iron ore in the Valley were abundant, and it was not long before other furnaces were built along the mountains to the west and to the east. I. D. McCauley, writing just one century ago, reflects the sanguine hopes of those days as he quotes an expert on mining:

> In his opinion, long before another generation shall have passed away, there will be dozens of furnaces and forges in our county, where now only one or two are to be found; that millions of dollars will be invested as soon as the trade of the country returns to its normal condition, where only thousands are now invested; and that long before the second centennial of our national existence shall have arrived, the development of the vast ore beds along the eastern and western borders of our valley will most inevitably make ours one of the very largest iron producing counties of the Commonwealth.[4]

This prediction, of course, never came true. The iron industry grew into a large business, but it gradually died when the rich ore deposits beyond the Great Lakes were discovered. Meanwhile the Chambers family was the largest mining proprietor of the Valley.

The last years of the war and the first years of the peace were a time of rampant inflation. The warring states taxed their citizens heavily, but even so there was never enough money to pay the bills. One of the soldiers' most common complaints was that they were not paid on time and frequently not at all. By the end of the war nearly every state was bankrupt or almost so, and suppliers in Europe and the West Indies were fearful that debts would never be paid—or, if paid, only in depreciated paper money. One historian states that one gold dollar would buy 40 paper dollars; another, that one dollar of specie was worth, in 1780, three thousand dollars of Continental currency.[5] "Not worth a Continental!" became a common way to describe anything that was worthless.

On 6 April 1781, the Assembly in Philadelphia, hoping to put an end to this frightful inflation, passed a law requiring the acceptance of paper money at face value. Robert Morris and General Mifflin fought the bill bitterly on the floor. They called it an ill-considered and deceptive bill that would only exacerbate the lamentable state of the currency. With tact yet with firmness, they said that the authors of the bill knew nothing of the intricacies of finance and should not attempt to guide the economy of the new Commonwealth. They pointed out that no law could command the confidence of the people in this currency and that the penalties included in the law were essentially unjust. They lost. The bill was passed. The result was a great wave of speculation that enriched many unscrupulous money-traders, mostly in the larger communities in the east, and impoverished thousands as the money they had grew of less value every day.

Everywhere the sorry economic position of the country caused concern, but the people of Franklin County and other rural districts suffered less from the appalling financial troubles of those years than did the city-dwellers. It is interesting that in the year of the Declaration of Independence, Adam Smith, a Scot of Edinburgh, published his famous book entitled *The Wealth of Nations,* in which he promulgated the economic doctrine of free trade. There should be a way out of the inflationary chaos. Adam Smith pointed the direction of the future.

The basis of wealth in the countryside was still agriculture. Its farms had long ago recovered from Indian depredations. New roads had made transport accessible. Moreover, there was throughout the countryside a feeling of security, a very different feeling from that of twenty or twenty-five years before. These people had never trusted the cities, and we have seen that the cities did very little to help them when they most needed help. They believed they could ride out the storm as they had done earlier. One heartening sign of future financial strength was the new furnace at Mount Pleasant.

Another favorable sign of the times was the arrival, over a span of a few years, of a handful of doctors of medicine. The first doctor to practice medicine in Franklin County was Dr. Hugh Mercer, who came to the site of the town that was later named for him in 1750. He was a friend of George Washington's and later a general in the Continental Army. He lost his life in the Battle of Princeton in 1777; whereupon the county in which

170

Princeton is situated was renamed Mercer County in his honor.

The first doctor in Chambersburg was Dr. John Calhoon, husband of Ruhamah Chambers, eldest daughter of Col. Benjamin Chambers. This couple lived for a time in a house where the Coyle Free Library now stands and in 1782 built the stone house which is now 297 Philadelphia Avenue. In 1781 Dr. Abraham Senseny, then a young man of twenty, opened his practice in Chambersburg and maintained it for 63 years, an amazing record. Two years later, on 1 January 1783, Dr. Alexander Stewart settled in Chambersburg. He was a native of Edinburgh and a graduate in medicine of the University of Edinburgh. He practised medicine for only ten years, dying in 1793. Dr. Andrew McDowell, born near Mercersburg and a scion of a family well known in the Valley, came to Chambersburg after his graduation from the University of Pennsylvania in 1787. He too, like Dr. Senseny, had a long term of years as a local physician, remaining in practice until his death in 1831. There were other physicians who came later—Dr. A. Clingman in 1788, Dr. Andrew Baum from 1790 to 1793, Dr. W. B. Scott from 1793 to 1805—but it was earlier men who most ministered to the needs of the community, delivered the babies and in some cases the children of those babies, and made it no longer necessary for Col. Chambers to administer home remedies to the ill.[6]

Chambersburg was a healthful community, thanks in large part to these conscientious physicians. There were no hospitals, no 'health services', no medical insurance, but there were clean air and pure water, healthy outdoor life, and a contagious feeling of physical and spiritual wellbeing. The worst lack was a dentist. It was only much later that the first dentist arrived in Chambersburg, but one must understand that in the eighteenth century an aching tooth was pulled at once and the words 'cavity' and 'filling' were not yet known. Few persons arrived at age 50 without a few gaps in their teeth; and then as now a severe toothache was considered about the worst affliction fate could visit upon a mortal man.

When Franklin County was carved out of Cumberland County by act of Assembly on 9 September 1784, certain changes were inevitable, Courts, for instance, would be held in the county seat. But as yet there was no court house; and thus, beginning on 15 September, the court met in an upstairs room of Jack's Tavern on the northwest corner of the square. Tradition says that on one occasion so many people crowded into the "court room" that the floor nearly gave way. The cellar of the tavern served for many years as a jail.

The history of the first true court house Chambersburg is interesting and carries with it a mystery. Col. Benjamin Chambers conveyed land on 28 September 1774 to Franklin Coun used as the site of a court house; and for this land, on which the present court house st received $26.66-2/3. Note that the land was con Franklin County ten years before that county being and before Chambersburg was delared t seat. Yet another ten years were to elapse befor Benjamin Chambers, grandson of the founder, first court house in 1794 at the cost of $41,00(only guess at the reason for this long delay, bu likely that Col. Chambers and other

ague Settlement expected that Franklin
'd be formed in 1774 or soon thereafter and
ation was not realized because of the war
ɪɔ..owed swiftly. Still, we do not know why the first
court house, for which land had been deeded twenty
years before, was not built until 1794.

The first court house, when finally built, was a two-
story brick structure with a gallery at the upper level. It
stood on a site immediately in front of the present court
house; and it was heated by two iron stoves large enough
to hold a full cord of wood. A prison of sorts was built
about 1791 on the northeast corner of Lincoln Way East
and Second Street.[7]

In the early life of the county it appears that most of
the cases tried or adjudicated in the court had to do with
property disputes, wills and bequests, petty larcenies,
and assault and battery. There were few instances of
serious crimes such as arson, burglary, or robbery. There
were two murder convictions in 1785 and one for rape in
1788 when a negro slave, "valued at $80," was con-
victed.[8] The people of the county were religious and law-
abiding folk; but more than once 'frontier justice', swift
and uncompromising, must have spared the courts.

The first elections in the new county were held
within a month of its establishment, on 12 October 1784.

At the time of the organization of our county,
the State Constitution of 1776 was in force. This
constitution provided that the Commonwealth
should be apportioned for representatives in the
General Assembly every seven years. They were to
be elected annually and could not serve more than
four years in seven.

The first election in our county was held on

FIRST *COURT HOUSE* FRANKLIN CO.,
BUILT IN 1784, REMOVED 1842.

Tuesday, October 12, 1784, in Chambersburg. This was the only voting place in the county and all who wished to vote had to come here.

The county was entitled to three representatives in the Legislature. The first Representatives elected were: James Johnston, Abraham Smith, and James McCalmont, all well known to any local historian.

By the Act of the 13th of September 1785, our county was divided into two election districts. The first district composed of the townships of Antrim, Peters, Guilford, Lurgan, Hamilton, Letterkenny, Franklin or Chambersburg, Washington, Southampton and Montgomery to vote at the Court House in Chambersburg. Fannett Township, the second district, was to vote at the house of the Widow Elliott in Fannett Township.

By an Act of the 10th of September 1787, our county was divided into four election districts. The first district composed of the townships of Guilford, Franklin, Hamilton, Letterkenny, Lurgan, and Southampton voted at the Court House in Chambersburg. The second district, Fannett, voted at the house of the Widow Elliott. The third district composed of Antrim and Washington Townships voted at the house of George Clark in Greencastle. The fourth district, Peters and Montgomery, voted at the house of James Crawford in Mercersburg. How different this was from our recent election with seventy election districts!

Our forefathers were able to vote only with time, trouble, and expense. They had to travel many miles over poor, often almost impassable roads and ford streams in order to cast their ballots . . .

By 1790 we had these election districts: Chambersburg, Strasburg, Fannett, Metal, Mercersburg, Greencastle, and Waynesboro.[9]

We have already written of some of our early churches: the Presbyterian Church of the Falling Spring, the First Evangelical Lutheran Church, Zion Reformed Church, Rocky Spring Church and the church at Grindstone Hill. We have almost heard the voice of the Rev. John Steele preaching from the pulpit at Church Hill near Mercersburg. Mennonite churches also dotted the Valley by the end of the eighteenth century. Episcopalians were then few, but they were cared for by the Rev. Thomas Barton, an itinerant clergyman who visited the Conococheague Settlement four times a year from 1755 onward. He was a loyalist and during the Revolution was imprisoned in his home in Lancaster for two years before being released to the British in 1778.[10]

A Covenanter church was organized in the town of Scotland by Alexander Thompson on 17 August 1791, and other similar churches were to be found later at Fayetteville and Greenwood Hill.[11] The Methodist Church, first introduced into America at Baltimore on 25 December 1784, was represented by a meeting house in Path Valley in 1799.[12]

Corpus Christi Church also belongs to the last years of the century. At first there were few Roman Catholics in or near Chambersburg, but by 1785 or a few years earlier their number had grown large enough to warrant periodic visits by itinerant Roman Catholic priests who ministered to them in their homes. There is a tradition that Corpus Christi Church was organized in 1785 or 1787. This may well be true; but the first church is known to have been built in 1792 on a lot purchased from Thomas Hartley, Esq. It was first called Christ's Church but later Corpus Christi Church. Like other early churches in the Valley, it was built of logs, 20' x 40' in size and 12' by 15' high. The first priest was the Rev. Dennis Cahill.[13]

At the very end of the eighteenth century—beyond the boundaries of this narrative, yet germane to it—there sprang up at Snow Hill in Washington township a religious society different from any other in the county. Peter Miller, a disciple of Johann Conrad Beissel of the Ephrata Cloister, converted Andrew Schneeberg (= Snow Hill) to the religious beliefs of the Seventh Day Baptists. Schneeberg was uneasy at first, but he finally established the Snow Hill branch of the Order of the Solitary at his home. Thus the Valley received its first and only monastic-conventual order.

The Constitutional Convention

The year 1787 was critical for the new republic for reasons known to everyone. A convention of delegates met in Philadelphia in May, instructed to consider revising the Articles of Confederation, which were patently ineffectual as an instrument of government.* Yet it was clear, even before the delegates met, that the major question would not be the revision of the Articles but rather the question whether circumstances now demanded a strong central government. So abhorrent was this idea to Patrick Henry that he refused to attend; and since Thomas Jefferson was then in Paris, Virginia was not represented at the convention.

The representatives of the other twelve states had also lesser yet important matters to consider. What, for

*Appendix K

177

instance, of the West? Congress had ordered that new states be admitted to the Union on an equal footing with the original thirteen when the new state had 60,000 or more free inhabitants. How might this ruling affect the economic and social balance of the new country?

Still the main topic was the question of a stronger central government, and into this debate was drawn the redoubtable Indian-fighter and Revolutionary soldier, James McCalmont. The Pennsylvania Legislature was meeting concurrently with the Constitutional Convention. The main question before the Legislature was whether a state convention should be called to ratify or reject the constitution which the Convention was expected at any moment to present to the country. But the Convention had not quite finished its work, though copies of the new constitution had leaked out; and thus the debate in the Legislature was clouded with uncertainty and marked by many expressions of strong feeling. One of those who felt most strongly was James McCalmont, a representative from Franklin County.

After nearly four months (May 24 - September 17), the great secret was now out. The document was eagerly read. Very many people in Pennsylvania, as well as other parts of the country, were astounded. The delegates to the convention had exceeded their instructions. Instead of revising the Articles of Confederation, they had produced an entirely new creature to rule over them. Rather than one legislative body, a regulation of nearly a century in Pennsylvania, a senate was added, composed of the "well-born," elected for six years in ways remote from control by the people. Besides, there was to be a president, elected for four years, with power to veto the will of the people as expressed in the legislature, their representatives, and nothing said about successive terms in that office. This seemed to be a sure road to dictatorship. — — The proposed constitution was silent about trial by jury, freedom of speech, et cetera. The opposition looked upon it as being preposterous. Because it had not been authorized, it was illegal, worthy of no serious consideration. This sentiment prevailed pretty generally in Franklin County and other sections in the central and western parts of the state.

In 1787, Pennsylvania had eighteen counties, seven having been ordained since 1776: Washington (1781), Fayette (1783), Franklin (1784), Montgomery (1784), Dauphin (1785), Huntingdon (1786), Luzerne (1787). Eight of the eighteen counties were west of the Susquehanna River, and solidly opposed to the constitution. Opposition was also strong in sections east of the river. Only Philadelphia and environs were as strongly favorable. Differences in living conditions and business interests, noted in earlier paragraphs, explain this wide range in difference of sentiment.

September 29, 1787 had been set by the Pennsylvania legislature as the day for final adjournment. About 4:00 o'clock in the afternoon of the 28th, motion was made and duly seconded that a state convention be called for ratification or rejection of the new constitution. Constitution opponents strongly objected:

1. The legislature had not been officially notified that a constitution had been made. Therefore it was very unparliamentary to

take any action at that time.

2. There should be a referendum, giving the people the opportunity to decide whether or not they wanted a convention for that purpose.

3. So much unfinished business was on the calendar that adjournment *sine die* could not be had the next day if due consideration was given to the motion.

These arguments fell on deaf ears. The opponents then filibustered until adjournment for the day was had, with the understanding that the convention question should be the first order of business the next day.

That night, nineteen opposing members met in Alexander Boyd's boarding house, on N. 6th St., a popular home for out-of-the-city members, for the purpose of deciding upon a program of strategy that would defeat the question the next day. Going over the probable vote, it seemed that the motion would carry. Whereupon, they agreed to remain away from the meeting, thereby breaking a quorum. This was done. At roll call on the 29th, but forty-five were present, two short of a quorum. The president directed the sergeant of arms to summons the absent members to be attendant to their legislative duty. This he did, but they refused to obey. Reporting this fact to the president, he was then directed to arrest two members, and bring them by force, if necessary, into the House. In the execution of this order, Jacob Miley, a member from Dauphin, and James McCalmont, a member from Franklin, were arrested. Miley seems to have gone along peaceably enough, but McCalmont, an Irish Indian fighter from Upper

Strasburg, proved to be a tough prisoner. He violently resisted arrest. Readily enough, idle loiterers in the vicinity of McCalmont's boarding house on N. Sixth St., assisted the officer in dragging him, fighting all the way, through the streets to Carpenter's Hall where the legislature was sitting. Bloody, with little clothing remaining on him, McCalmont was finally forced into his seat.

The president then announced a quorum was present, and the House prepared for the transaction of business. McCalmont promptly arose, said he was present under most trying circumstances, and wished to retire. The president refused the request on the grounds that the member was in contempt to the House for violating its rules by breaking a quorum through absence. Therefore, he was fined five shillings as fixed by the rules. Immediately, McCalmont took five shillings out of his pocket and said: "Here's your money. Now let me go." The president decided the money could not be received because the rules said nothing about payment of the fine. He further explained that, since the fine had been duly imposed, the member was now purged of his contempt, and might duly participate in the business of the House. He regretted it was not possible to excuse the member from attendance at that time, because consideration to be given important business demanded a quorum.

At this, McCalmont again arose, claimed his privilege as a member to leave the room at his pleasure, and started toward the door. Other members shouted, "Stop him", and forced him back into his seat. McCalmont, still undaunted, asked for a resolution by the House, excusing him from further attendance. By this time, many of the members seemed to have become ashamed of what was going on, and sympathy was running strongly for McCalmont, even from the pro-constitution contingent. Accordingly, motion was made and seconded that McCalmont be excused. In the debate of the motion, many members spoke in very apologetic tone, but voiced opposition to the motion for the same reasons that the president had given for his refusal to grant permission to retire. Others thought, under the circumstances, he ought to be allowed to go. When put, the motion was lost by almost unanimous (*viva voce*) vote.

Thereupon, the original question of the previous day, authorizing a state convention to take action on the proposed constitution, was put, and carried by the vote of 30 to 15. McCalmont and his colleague from Franklin County, Abraham Smith, voted against it. — — Just before this vote was taken, a messenger rushed into the House, bearing official proclamation from the national congress, announcing the Constitution, and calling upon the states for due action toward ratification or rejection. Thus, in the nick of time, the pro-constitution members in the legislature were given fair ground to stand upon in their demand for a ratifying convention.[14]

Thus do we say farewell to one of the most colorful figures we have encountered in this narrative. As he had fought the Indians and the British, so McCalmont fought for his own opinions in the Legislature and yielded only to *force majeure*. We know little of his remaining years except that he died on 19 July 1809, aged 70, and was buried in the burying ground beside the Rocky Spring Church where throughout his lifetime he had occupied Pew 25.[15]

As for the new Constitution, we know that it was ratified within a year by eleven states, Rhode Island and North Carolina standing aside for a time. Pennsylvania ratified it on 12 December 1787 by a vote of 46 to 23. It went into effect on the first Wednesday of March, 1789, and in that year received its first ten amendments, the so-called Bill of Rights. George Washington was inaugurated as first President in the new Federal Hall in New York on 30 April. It is interesting that six days later the Estates General met in Paris and on 14 July the mob stormed the Invalides for arms and the Bastille for powder. Hardly had one revolution settled down before another burst into life. Both exerted a more profound effect on the future of the western world than any person then alive could have foreseen.

Chambersburg and the county around it were now prospering despite a still uncertain and wavering currency. In 1787 Captain Benjamin Chambers built a large three-story house on what is now called the Rosedale Theatre lot on North Main Street. It was "built on the old English style . . with tall chimneys, deep dormer windows . . . walls covered with ivy. . . extensive grounds . . garden in front . . choice flowers . . roses from front door to street": hence the name Rosedale.[16] Col. Chambers completed the handsome stone house on the hill, the second building north of the manse of the Falling Spring Church, incorporating in its south wall stones from the now defunct fort.

The tax assessment lists for the year 1786 bear evidence of much comfortable wealth in Franklin County and suggest where some of it came from:

Horses	3324	Fulling mills	3
Cows	4141	Hemp and oil mills	4
Slaves	227	Stills	96
Grist Mills	40	Iron works	2
Saw mills	32	Tan yards	13

In Chambersburg there were 96 improved lots and 40 unimproved; in Greencastle, 37 improved and 21 unimproved. Antrim township shows the highest assessment and Franklin township the least, being the smallest.

Two years later, in Franklin township (Chambersburg) only, the assessment list shows the following:

Improved lots	134 (38 more than in 1786)		
Unimproved lots	24 (16 fewer than in 1786)		
Horses	105		
Cows	126	Slaves	18 (2 fewer than in 1786)
Oxen	4	Servants	6
Bulls	1	Chair	1 (there is some mystery about this lone chair)

In that year there were four physicians, three attorneys, four merchants, four justices of the peace and *ex officio* judges of the courts, and twelve innkeepers. The population in 1786 was approximately 526 and in 1788, 804.[17]

Some will be surprised by the number of slaves shown in these tabulations. On 1 March 1780, the Commonwealth of Pennsylvania passed "An Act for the Gradual Abolition of Slavery". Obviously this act did not at once eliminate slavery, but it helped create an anti-slavery opinion which in turn produced conditions favorable enough to attract many blacks fleeing from the southern slave states.[18] The last slave auction in Franklin County occurred in 1828.

184

Some will also have noticed with surprise that in 1788 Chambersburg had three times as many innkeepers as physicians or merchants and four times as many as attorneys. The reason is not far to seek. There were as yet no public buildings; we have already noticed that the first courts were held in Jack's Tavern. The twelve inns on the assessment list were the meeting-places for formal assemblies of this sort, for business appointments, for political meetings, and of course for exchange of news. There was no Samuel Johnson in the "Cheshire Cheese," little enough talk of plays and poems, no sophistication and polish. But there was wholesome food and abundant drink, and the local inhabitants as well as the stray traveller got a fair return for their money. Moreover, when the citizens flocked into Chambersburg to vote, many had to spend the night in town and nearly all had to eat at least one meal. All the taverns were crowded on election day.

There is extant information about five of these taverns in addition to Jack's. Directly across the street from Jack's was the Green Tree Hotel, built about 1786 and standing on the present site of the Central Presbyterian Church. A few doors south, on the west side of Main Street, was William Morrow's tavern, now designated by a historical marker. In 1777 Nicholas Snyder opened a tavern on the east side of North Main Street a few doors from the square; later this enterprise was conducted by Jacob Snyder and others. Farther down South Main Street, Michael Trout was proprietor of the Indian Queen Hotel; and west of the Conococheague stood Miller's Hotel.[19] Thus there were six taverns or hotels on the square or within a stone's throw of it.

As for the 96 stills, they would appear adequate to supply the taverns and hotels. At that time nearly every substantial farm had its own still, and many were to be found beside grist mills. It is only fair to say that the 96 were the acknowledged and taxed stills; how many illicit stills were hidden away in the mountains no man knows.

Two new evidences of the growth and importance of Chambersburg belong to the year 1788. This year saw the founding of the first paper mill in the Valley by John Scott. His mill produced writing and printing paper. For eight years the newspapers of Pittsburgh and other communities west of the mountains were supplied by John Scott & Co. On 20 May Congress established the post road from Philadelphia to Pittsburgh. Chambersburg was made a way-station and thus immediately gained new prominence. The post passed through ''once in each fortnight''.[20]

At about this time it appears that Col. Chambers's mill ceased operation.[21] It may have worn out. Or it may have given way to growing competition; we have seen that in 1786 there were 40 grist mills and 32 saw mills in the county. More likely the family interests were now centered in the iron mill a few miles from Fort Loudon. Here was now the source of wealth; mining, not milling, was the coming thing.

While the silence of the millstones and waterwheel of Col. Chambers's mill must have brought an inevitable note of sadness to Franklin County and marked the end of the first industry established in the Valley, Col. Chambers's death in this year 1788 marked the end of an era. He was laid to rest in the burying-ground that he had conveyed to the Presbyterian Church of the Falling Spring many years before, and above his grave stands now a monument, simple and in perfect taste, bearing this epitaph:

In Memory of
Col. Benjamin Chambers
First White Settler of
Franklin County in 1730
Founder of Chambersburg
and
Donor of These Grounds
To the Presbyterian Church
in 1768
Who died in 1788
Aged 80 years
Also His Wife
Jane Williams Chambers
Who Died in 1795
Aged 70 Years[22]

This is indeed a simple and modest statement, this epitaph. The founder of Chambersburg, of course. But also its first citizen throughout the 58 years of his life in the community he founded and fostered; the first man to build a saw mill and a grist mill; colonel in the militia organized to protect the people; magistrate who administered the laws and did not shirk the hard duty that gave the Valley the name of Burnt Cabins; friend of the Indians at first and always understanding toward them even as he prepared his fort to ward off their attacks; stubborn enough to resist when authorities demanded his swivel guns; agent of the Propietors in their quarrel with Maryland over the border with Pennsylvania; generous benefactor of three churches and loyal member of one; father of a thriving family of children who bore the name proudly and with merit for generations thereafter; healer of illnesses and drawer of teeth in the first years; jack of all trades; honest, trustworthy, friendly, admired by all for his virtues and—so far as we know—hated by none: this was a man who may stand as the very epitome of the adventurous spirit and the physical and spiritual stamina of the early pioneers of the frontier.

His life encompassed not only the founding of the Conococheague Settlement but also the Seven Years' War, the laying out of Chambersburg, the formation of Franklin County, the War of Independence, and the Constitutional Convention. He had come as a young man to a remote confluence of two streams, unpeopled by white men, on a frontier hardly recognized as existing by the Proprietors in the east. When he died, the dangerous frontier was secure, the confluence was a village, the territory a county, and the province a Commonwealth within a free and independent country. The heart of this great and good man must have rejoiced many times that he was permitted to play such a vital part in the founding and growth of this community and that he had lived to see so many changes, ending in a new country and a new citizenship under a flag bearing a circle of thirteen stars in its crest. We may say of him, as Wordsworth said of Milton,

> Pure as the naked heavens, majestic, free,
> So didst thou travel on life's common way,
> In cheerful godliness; and yet thy heart
> The lowliest duties on herself did lay.

The rhythm of events in Chambersburg and Franklin County is interesting. We have witnessed a period of about 25 years of settlement and quiet growth. Then comes a decade of troubles with the Indians, followed by another decade or so of peace and prosperity. Yin and Yang. Then comes another period of less than ten years, the years of the Revolutionary War. There was peace again for about another decade; and then the brief fireworks described in the Epilogue.

It is impossible to read a philosophy of history out of this sequence of events. What stands forth most prominently and unmistakably, however, is the resilience of the inhabitants of Franklin County and of the Cumberland Valley generally—resilience supplementing the energy and endurance described in the Foreword. During the Indian troubles, the men of the Valley were in no mood to build, clear land, and expand their holdings. Their aim in those years was solely to hold on to what they had and beat off the danger. Ten years later they responded to the call to arms and the county was stripped of its men of young and middle age. Again it was a matter of holding on until hostilities should cease and the men return.

But when they did, in 1781 and the years following, Franklin County and the Cumberland Valley embarked on a period of phenomenal growth, partially traced in this chapter. Neither the Indian Terror nor the hardships and inflation of the Revolutionary years had damped the spirits of these people. They had suffered, yes; but with resilience of body and mind they overcame their troubles and patiently and resolutely continued to build a new civilization along the frontier—a frontier now receding ever westward. With minor fluctuations of fortune, this growth continued unabated until the years of the Civil War, 1861-65.

EPILOGUE

One hesitates to add anything to this tale after the death of Col. Benjamin Chambers, whose life encloses it like a great parenthesis. There is one more important incident, however, that we should record if only because it brings back onto the Chambersburg stage the Colonel's son James, whom we have lost to sight for some years. The warrior of the family had lived quietly in his growing community, buying land from his father and laying out streets in the southern part of Chambersburg and naming Catherine Street after his wife; and gradually assuming the leadership of the Chambers family and the position of first citizen long held by his now deceased father. He was one of the judges of the county courts and a County Commissioner, 1793-96. He was to play a part in the Whiskey Rebellion that came to a climax in 1794. [*]

Excise laws were never popular in colonial days. The Pennsylvania Assembly passed one in 1738 but soon repealed it under widespread popular pressure. This performance was exactly repeated six years later, in 1744. The excise law of 1772 had a better fate. Everyone could see that the government needed money badly; and though enforcement was lax, money was raised and mercifully—from the government's point of view— continued to be raised throughout most of the war years. Then this law also was repealed. [1]

Again in 1791 the government—now under a new name—passed an excise law.

> The new Federal government, being sadly in need of revenue, had passed among other acts an excise law, imposing a tax of two pence a quart on spirituous liquors. It will be noticed that although

[*]Appendix   L

190

dollar currency had already been established, it was still the custom to reckon in English money and the tax was equivalent to about 8 cents a gallon . . . .

At that time packhorses were the only means of transportation across the mountains. One horse could carry four bushels of rye, but if reduced by distillation one horse could carry two kegs of whiskey containing eight gallons each, the product of 24 bushels.[2]

But the Scotch-Irish people of the western counties of Pennyslvania opposed the tax bitterly.

There had been much opposition to the imposition of an excise tax on distilled liquors from the earliest days of the Province. Our Scotch and Scotch-Irish ancestors knew what the imposition and collection of such a tax meant in the Fatherland. The most outrageous exactions and impositions had been practiced upon them there, and they doubtless were resolved to prevent a like occurrence. They knew how to distill the spirits, had the means and appliances to produce the drink, and were determined to use the product of their stills. Hence they were outspoken in their opposition to the tax, and did all that was in their power to render the act nugatory, and the position of inspector and collector of the excise a most undesirable and dangerous one for any man to fill.

The people of Western Pennsylvania also complained that they had suffered much from the depreciation of the currency of the country, whether colonial, provincial or confederate; that they were located on the borders of civilization, far removed from the markets and exchanges on the sea-board; that their agricultural products would not bear the cost of transportation to a market; that they had no means to buy salt, iron and steel; and that their principal cereal (rye) could not be utilized unless distilled into whiskey, for which it was specially adapted, making the best product, which was always and universally in demand.[3]

"In addition to all this," writes S. G. Fisher, "the French Revolution was at that time in its fiercest throes of insanity. Its wild ideas had penetrated the Alleghenies and for a moment had over-excited the generous impulses and unseated the steady reason of the Scotchmen."[4] Moreover, the rise in prices during the French Revolution had greatly enriched the farmers of the east but not yet those in the west; and this discrepancy irked the westerners.

It was not only a matter of using their grain advantageously; it was also a matter of reaping a large profit, for the whiskey doubled in sales value by the time it reached the eastern seaboard. And so the dissidents in the west held meetings—one of them was said to have assembled some 7,000 men—and drew up a resolution on 22 August 1792 which they forwarded to Congress. They demanded repeal of the obnoxious law and refused all cooperation with the tax-collectors. It was downright rebellion.

Always hoping for moderation and unwilling to invoke military measures until all else failed, Washington, on 15 September, issued a proclamation "exhorting . . all persons . . to desist from unlawful combinations intended to obstruct the operation of the laws."[5] When there was no perceptible response in the west,

Governor Millfin, in a message to the Legislature on 7 December, at last threatened the use of force.

Matters dragged on in this way for more than a year. No one wished to force the issue. The westerners believed that Governor Mifflin was bluffing and had little fear that President Washington would wish to burden the slender treasury of the United States with the cost of a military expedition across the Alleghenies. Swallowing his threats for a moment, Governor Mifflin appointed a commission of prominent citizens on 6 August 1794 to visit the western counties and promise the dissidents oblivion of past disturbances in return for future obedience to the law. On the next day- -possibly there was collusion betwęen the Governor and the President— Washington issued another proclamation calling for obedience and on 8 September appointed a Federal commission of three men to aid and abet the labors of the State commission. He promised oblivion but implied clearly that this was to be the last such offer and henceforth offenders would "not be protected from the operation of the law".[6] The two commissions worked together to convince the men of the west that law was a better guide than emotion, but the only reply of the dissidents was a long bill of complaints against the Federal government.

These disturbances made little noise in distant New England, which doubtless accounts for the slight mention of them in the works of some of our New England historians. But Washington faced a dilemma: either he had to move firmly and put down the insurrection or he had to hide behind his genuine desire for a peaceful outcome and find a formula which in modern jargon would be called appeasement.

His solution was to instruct the Secretary of War, General Henry Knox, to call upon the governors of four states—Pennsylvania, New Jersey, Maryland, and Virginia—for an aggregate of 12,950 troops. Those from Pennsylvania and New Jersey were to gather at Carlisle, the others at Cumberland. The quota for Pennsylvania was the largest of the four, 5,200 men; and the quota for Franklin County was 281.

It was a bold act, and like most bold acts by statesmen drew widespread opposition, especially in western and central Pennsylvania. It is easy to understand why many citizens of the Cumberland Valley sympathized with the insurgents. A large number of them were Scotch-Irishmen, Presbyterians, descendants of settlers who had faced the same demanding frontier life. Nor may we forget the 96 stills listed in Franklin County six years ago. The whiskey produced in Franklin County was also liable to the unpopular tax.

And so there were riots and "Liberty Poles" in the Valley: on 8 September in Carlisle; a few days later in Chambersburg and Greencastle. The pole was strung with bunting, placed in a prominent position in each town, and crowned with a placard which read "Liberty and No Excise on Whiskey!" Col. James Chambers, soon to be promoted to the grade of Brigadier-General for his services in the Insurrection, was absent from home when the Liberty Pole was erected in Chambersburg. On 22 September he wrote this letter to A. J. Dallas, Secretary of the Commonwealth:

On the 16th inst. I arrived in Chambersburg, and to my great astonishment I found the Rabble had raised what they Caled a Liberty pole. Some of the most active of the inhabitants was at the time absent, and upon the whole, perhaps, it was best, as matters has Since taken a violent change. When I came hear I found the magistrates had opposed the sitting of the pole up, to the utmost of their power, but was not Supported by the majority of Cittyzens. They wished to have the Royators Subject to Law, and (Mr. Justice John Riddle, John Scott and Christian Oyster) the magistrates of this place informed me of the zealous wish to have them brought to Justice. I advised them to Call a meeting of the inhabitants of the town on the next morning, and we would have the matter opened to them, and Show the necessity of Soporting Government, Contrassed with the destruction of one of the best governments in the world.

The meeting was held in the "Coorthous"— Mr. John Riddle delivered a very animating address to the people—Resolves were passed and drawn up for the people to sign, pledging them to support the Justices in their efforts "to bring the Royators to tryal," and General Chambers continues: I am now happy to have in my power to request you, Sir, to inform his Excellency, the Govenour, that these exertions has worked the desired Change. The magistrates has sent for the men, the very Same that Errected the pole, and I had the pleasure of Seeing them, on Saturday evening, Cut it down; and with the Same waggon that brought it into town, they were oblidgeed to draw the remains of it out of town again. The Circumstance was mortifying, and they behaived very well. They seem very penetant, and no person offered them any insult. It has worked such a change. I believe we will be able Shortly to Send our Quota to Carlisle.[7]

Perhaps it was this decisive action that made it possible for Col. James to fill his quota of 281 men in spite of the local opposition to the excise law and to the military expedition.

Thus the troops were streaming into Carlisle, Col. James and his 'quota' among them. Washington arrived on 4 October.

On October 1, 1794 General Thomas Mifflin, Governor of the Commonwealth, arrived at Carlisle, at the head of the Pennsylvania troops called to assist in quelling the "Whiskey Insurrection," and in the evening he delivered an animated address in the Presbyterian Church. On the 4th, General Washington, President of the United States, accompanied by General Alexander Hamilton, Secretary of the Treasury, who was also his private secretary, a large company of soldiers, a great number of the yeomanry and members of General Assembly, arrived in the town, all on their way westward. It was the most illustrious group of Americans ever assembled in the interior of the Commonwealth on any occasion.[8]

After eight days of reviewing his troops and completing preparations, General Washington gave orders to begin the march west. Both cavalry and infantry proceeded together as far as Shippensburg; the infantry then moved by way of Strasburg, the cavalry to Chambersburg. A pleasing account of the early portion of the cavalry march comes from the personal journal of a certain Captain Ford, who commanded a company from New Jersey.

October 11 (Carlisle).—This day we parade for

marching. Was joined by the Pennsylvania horse, and after saluting the President, marched on to Mount Rock.

October 12.—Marched for Shippensburg; the cavalry by themselves. This day we passed one of the largest springs, which turned several mills in a few rods from its source, and in three miles there was a number of other mills. This town is pleasantly situated, consists of about two hundred houses and belongs to the Shippens in Philadelphia, put out on perpetual leases, on a moderate quit-rent.

October 13.—The cavalry themselves marched for Chambersburg, a pleasant village consisting of about two hundred houses, much better built than Shippensburg. This town lays (sic) on the waters of the famous Conogocheche, near where it was proposed to have the final seat of federal government, and is the county town of _____; has a very handsome court house, a market and some capital mills, and belongs to Captain Chambers, who has leased on moderate terms. This town has risen suddenly, not having been laid out more than ten years; here we found the best tavern we had seen for a long time. Captain Chambers was so polite as to invite me, with General White's family, to dine with him.

October 14—Halted this day to give the Pennsylvanians an opportunity to vote for congress and assemblymen. The country down this valley is very fine and good.[9]

The General and his entourage put up at the Morrow Tavern, a few doors south of the square. It is not clear whether they spent one or two nights in

Chambersburg. The letter quoted above would suggest two.

Now occurs an incident that belongs to Greencastle but cannot be omitted here if only because it is one of the rare moments of humor that the stern events of these years have left us:

At daylight on Monday morning, October 13th, he left Chambersburg. The people were at their doors and the President acknowledged their salutations as he rode along the street on horseback. He was followed by his black servant carrying a large portmanteau.

In a few hours the party reached Greencastle and stopped for breakfast in a house on the southeast corner of the Public Square. This tavern was kept by Robert McCulloh. An incident occurred here which has often been told and is worth telling again: While the General and his friends were at breakfast McCulloh's son Tom, a boy about ten years of age, anxious to be close to these men, found his way into the room and under the table. He was soon discovered by his father, who sternly commanded him to come out and leave the room, with the promise of being well-punished. General Washington interfered and with a few kindly words patted the boy on the head who was then allowed to remain in the room. He often referred to his unpleasant position under the table among the big boots and spurs of the company. This lad, Thomas G. McCulloh, grew up and became one of Franklin County's leading attorneys and represented this district in the Sixteenth Congress. He was the first president of the Cumberland Valley Railroad.[10]

The remainder of this unique event—except for Shay's Rebellion in Massachusetts in 1786-87 against the foreclosure of mortgages and the effects of depreciated currency, it was the first popular revolt against Federal authority—can be told in a few words. The little army arrived in Pittsburgh on 17 November. The dissidents, impressed by the fact that Washington had actually carried out his plan, chose to accept the new law (which was speedily revised so as to be less onerous) and no shot was fired. The troops turned around and marched for home, reaching Carlisle on 10 December. Even the New Jersey troops were home for Christmas.

There are two prevailing opinions about the Whiskey Rebellion. One, quite commonly held, is to be found in an essay on George Washington by our local historian, A. J. White Hutton,[11] who believed that the rebellion had been dignified out of all proportion to its true importance; that it had significance only because it occurred when the Federal government was new and unsure; and that Washington's participation in this *opéra bouffe* gave it far more luster than it deserved.

The other, even more commonly held, is expressed by George Chambers, grandson of the founder:

> The civil authority was found totally incompetent to execute the laws and maintain the public peace. There was no alternative left to the Executive government but a choice between submission to lawless combinations against the government and laws, or to execute the laws passed by the Representatives of the people, in conformity to the Constitution, with all the powers confided to the Chief Magistrate of the Republic.

The National government, under the Federal constitution, was then in its infancy: an experiment on trial; but fortunately for the country, at such a crisis, Washington was at the head of the government. Whilst the President took measures to call out the militia to suppress the insurrection, he expressed his deep regret at the occasion, but with the most solemn conviction, that the essential interests of the Union demanded it, that the very existence of the government and the fundamental principles of social order were involved in the issue, the insurgents were by proclamation, required to disperse and retire to their respective homes.

The President though firm and decided to execute the laws and maintain the government, made, in the midst of preparation for military organization, a peaceful effort to bring the disaffected to a sense of their duty, appointing three commissioners of talents and integrity, to repair to the scene of insurrection and confer with them, promising amnesty in case of submission to the laws. In this they were unsuccessful, and the President was under the painful necessity of putting the military force in motion.[12]

And thus with President Washington's arrival in Franklin County, his Presidential progress through it, and his departure from it, and with Col. James now a Brigadier-General and home from his last campaign, we bring this account to a conclusion. The final words may be taken from the legend surrounding the pyramid on the back of the dollar bill of today, the Bicentennial Year. The peak of the pyramid is raised above the body of it, is surrounded by a divine effulgence, and contains the all-seeing eye of God, who appears to approve of what he sees. The legend reads:

Novus Ordo Seclorum Annuit Coeptis
A new order of the centuries gives the nod to things begun.

It is not very good Latin, but it points to a future for Chambersburg, for Franklin County, and for the nation.

FOOTNOTES

FOREWORD

[1]Bambrick, Col. W. C., "Scotland Village," *KHSP*, X, 26

PROLOGUE

[1]Fisher, S. G., *The Making of Pennsylvania*, Philadelphia: Lippincott, 1896, 1924, 1932, Preface, iii

[2]Johnson, Paul, *Elizabeth I, A Biography*, New York: Holt, Rinehart & Winston, 1974, 384

[3]*ibid*, 378

[4]*ibid.*, 382. The poet Edmund Spenser was one of the first of these English settlers. Though a man of incorrigible optimism and good will, Spenser could speak only bitterly of the Irish.

[5]Mitchison, Rosalind, *A History of Scotland*, London: Methuen, 1970, 175

[6]*ibid.*, 197, 199

[7]Enc. Brit., "Ireland", 11th edition, 1910, XIV, 775

[8]Notestein, Wallace, *The Scot in History*, New Haven: Yale University Press, 1946, 58

[9]Benchoff, Lucy Chambers, "A Story of Colonial Times in Franklin County", *KHSP*, XIV, 331

[10]Guthrie, L. R., "The Scotch-Irish Stream of Migration, Its Source, Channels and Reservoirs," *KHSP*, X, 154

[11]Brereton, T. J., "Scenes and Incidents of the Cumberland Valley," *KHSP*, III, 47

[12]Fisher, S. G., *op cit*, 87. I am indebted to this volume for many facts about the Pennsylvania Germans.

[13]*ibid.*, 96-99

[14]Foltz, M. A., "The German Influence in Pennsylvania, with Special Reference to Franklin County," *KHSP*, I, 62

[15]*ibid.*, 73

[16]*ibid.*, 72-73

CHAPTER I: THE EARLY SETTLERS

[1]Orr, J. G., "Early Grist Mills of Lurgan Township," *KHSP*, III, 79-80

[2]*ibid.*, 87

[3]Fisher, S. G., *Pennsylvania: Colony and Commonwealth*, Philadelphia: Coates, 1897, 6-7

[4]This license empowered Benjamin Chambers to "take and settle and improve four hundred acres of land at the Falling Spring mouth, and on both sides of the Conocochege Creek, for the conveniency of a grist mill and plantation." McCauley, I. H., *Historical Sketch of Franklin County, Pennsylvania*, Chambersburg: D. F. Pursel, 1877-78, 9

[5]Stoner, J. H., "The Mason and Dixon Line", *KHSP*, X, 51-53

[6]*ibid.*, 55

[7]Seilhamer, G. O., "The Founders of Chambersburg," *KHSP*, I, 44-46

[8]Hutton, A. J. W., "The General Who Preferred to be Called Colonel," *KHSP*, XII, 248

[9]Emmons, H. H., "John Armstrong and His Descendants," *KHSP*, IX, 303

[10]See Rupp, I. D., *The History and Topography of Dauphin, Cumberland, Franklin, Bedford, Adams, and Perry Counties*, Lancaster: Gilbert Hills, 1846, 396, for a description of the medal presented to Col. John Armstrong by the Corporation of Philadelphia in gratitude for this brave and successful exploit.

[11]Seilhamer, G. O., "Old Conococheague Families." *KHSP*, II, 288

[12]Seilhamer, G. O., "The Men of Middle Spring," *KHSP*, III, 53

[13]See Green, J. R., *Short History of the English People*, New York: A. L. Burt Co., n.d., II, 340

[14]Deatrich, C. M., "Historical Sketch of Saint Thomas, Formerly Campbellstown," *KHSP*, IV, 244 and "The Campbells Are Coming," *KHSP*, IX, 179. The author states that in 1818 it was discovered that another Campbellstown was already in existence. The townsfolk proposed to rename the village as Thomas or Thomastown. As a jest—alluding slyly to the founder's rather rowdy ways—one member of the meeting offered an amendment: "let us call it *Saint* Thomas." The amendment was adopted.

[15]Rose, Rev. J. G., "The Welsh Run Church," *KHSP*, IX, 605

[16]Runk, J. M., "Pioneer Life and Pioneers of Franklin County," *KHSP*, IX, 46

[17]Nead, B. M. "James McLene," *KHSP*, VI, 38

[18]Orr, J. G., "Early Highways II", *KHSP*, IV, 237

[19]Foltz, M. A., "A Backward Glance at the Traits, Traditions and Personality of the Early Scotch-Irish," *KHSP*, II, 25

[20]Orr, J. G., "Culbertson's Row," *KHSP*, II, 123

[21]Burgner, M. K., "Major James McCalmont," *KHSP*, IX, 382

[22]Gillan, Hon. W. Rush, "Mary Jemison," *KHSP*, IX, 492

[23]Gillan, Hon. W. Rush, "The Wilson Family," *KHSP*, V, 200

[24]Thrush, Dr. A. W., "Along the Loudon Road II," *KHSP*, XI, 454

[25]Diehl, S. R., "An Old Home in Path Valley," *KHSP*, XIV, 130 Also D A B, VI, Part 2, 123-4

[26]Palmer, J. G., "The Evaluation of a Challenge," *KHSP*, XIII, 158

[27]*Early History of Waynesboro and Franklin County*, paper prepared by the late C. W. Cremer and read before the Kittochtinny Historical Society and the Franklin County Chapter of the Daughters of the American Revolution by R. C. Gordon, c. 1917, 5

[28]*History of Franklin County, Pennsylvania*, Chicago: Warner, Beers & Co., 1887, Chapter II

[29]Quoted by Davison, W. R., "Reminiscences of Greencastle," *KHSP*, IX, 535

[30]*Early History of Waynesboro*, 2

CHAPTER II: INDIAN TROUBLES

[1]For the anthropological background, see Dickson, Dr. J. A. "The Prehistoric American Indian of Eastern United States," *KHSP*, XV, 115

[2]After their defeat by the white man in the Carolinas in 1713, the Tuscaroras migrated northward and were accepted by the Iroquois. Thenceforward there were the Six Nations. In coming north, the Tuscaroras passed along the Tuscarora Path Valley, which we call now Path Valley.

[3]Ives, Major Chauncey, "The Indians of the Valley," *KHSP*, II, 43

[4]*ibid.*, 111

[5]*ibid.*, 107

[6]Burgner, M. K., "Major James McCalmont," *KHSP*, IX, 374

[7]Chambers, George, A *Tribute to the Principles, Virtues, Habits and Public Usefulness of the Irish and Scotch Early Settlers of Pennsylvania*, Chambersburg: M. A. Foltz, 1871, 28. It is probable that this 'walk' was conducted in the manner of an athletic contest

known, then and now, as the 'one-mile walk', the 'five-mile walk', etc. The contestants 'walked' without bending the knees, throwing their legs forward from the hip. The 'walker' could make good speed, but it was exhausting; and as we see, only one contestant had the stamina to finish. To the Indians, this kind of 'walk' would have been almost indistinguishable from running.

[8] Fisher, S. G. *Pennsylvania: Colony and Commonwealth*, Philadelphia: Coates, 1897, 118

[9] Chambers, *op. cit.*, 61

[10] Rupp, I. D., *The History and Topography of Dauphin, Cumberland, Franklin, Bedford, Adams and Perry Counties*, Lancaster: Gilbert Hills, 1846, 384

[11] Seilhamer, G. O., "Old Conococheague Families," *KHSP*, II, 295

[12] Hoerner, W. S., "The Colonial Defenses of Franklin County," *KHSP*, II, 12

[13] For a full account, see *The Frontier Forts of Pennsylvania*, Harrisburg, 1916, I, 472

[14] For an accurate and stirring account of this conflict, see Fiske, John, *New France and New England*, New York: Houghton, Mifflin & Co., 1904

[15] Orr, J. G., "Culbertson's Row," *KHSP*, II, 124

[16] *The Frontier Forts of Pennsylvania*, Harrisburg, 1916, I, 529-30

[17] Finafrock, J. L., "Church Hill," *KHSP*, XII, 214

[18] Rupp, I. D., *op. cit.*, 90

[19] *The Frontier Forts of Pennsylvania*, Harrisburg, 1916, I, 552-53

[20] Foreman, H. E., "The Story of the Fort," *KHSP*, XV, 50. See also *History of Franklin County, Pennsylvania*, Chicago: Warner, Beers & Co., 1887, 169

[21] For a full account of these forts, see *The Frontier Forts of Pennsylvania*, Harrisburg, 1916, passim and McCauley, I. H., *Historical Sketch of Franklin County, Pennsylvania*, Chambersburg: D. F. Pursell, 1877-78, 16 ff.

[22] *The Frontier Forts*, I, 509

[23] *ibid.*, I, 529

[24] *ibid.*, 530-31. Mrs. Lucy Chambers Benchoff believes that Col. Chambers had *four* swivels, two of which he bought in England and two of which were supplied by the province. She believes that the quarrel concerned the latter two.

[25] "James McCullough's Records of Indian Outrages," *KHSP*, IX, 459

[26] Stewart, Mrs. H. W., *History of the Cumberland Valley*, no p., c. 1917, 71-72

[27] Brereton, T. J., "Scenes and Incidents of the Cumberland Valley," *KHSP*, III, 51

[28] Montgomery, John, "Dr. Hugh Mercer and Col. Robert Magaw," *KHSP*, III, 132

[29] Fisher, S. G., *op. cit.*, 184-87

[30] Kauffman, M. E., "War Trails to the Conococheague Settlements," *KSHP*, XV, 112-13

[31] "James McCullough's Record of Indian outrages" taken from *Loudon's Narratives*, Carlisle, 1811, and reprinted in *KHSP*, IX, 459

[32] McKnight, Charles, *Our Western Border One Hundred Years Ago*, Philadelphia McCurdy, 1879, 4-5

CHAPTER III: PONTIAC'S WAR

[1] Churchill, Sir Winston, *The Age of Revolution*, New York: Dodd, Mead & Co., 1957, 161; being Volume III of the series entitled *A History of the English-Speaking Peoples*.

²Fisher, *op. cit.*, 222

³*ibid.*, 240

⁴McKnight, *op. cit.*, 180-81

⁵Prisoners: male, Indian over 10, 150 pieces of eight
male, Indian 10 or younger; female Indian over 10, 130 pieces of eight

Scalps: male, over 10, 134 pieces of eight
female over 10, 50 pieces of eight

Quoted from Webster, Eleanor M., "The Insurrection at Fort Loudon in 1765: Rebellion or Preservation of Peace?" *Western Pennsylvania Historical Magazine*, Vol. 47, No. 2, April 1964, 127

⁶Fisher, *op. cit.*, 237

⁷*op. cit.*, 72-75

⁸*op. cit.*, 76-78

⁹Quoted in *History of Franklin County, Pennsylvania*, Chicago: Warner, Beers & Co., 1887, I, 172

¹⁰Webster, Eleanor M., *op. cit.*, 139; quoted from Smith, James, *Incidents of Border Life*, Chambersburg: J. Pritts Co., 1839

¹¹Seilhamer, G. O., "Some Missing and Misplaced Ancestors," *KHSP*, V, 261

¹²Mowrey, R. G., "Franklin County References in Selected Fact and Fiction," *KHSP*, XIV, 178

¹³Webster, E. M., *op. cit.*, 138-39

¹⁴Hoerner, W. S., "The Colonial Defenses of Franklin County," *KSHP*, II, 47

CHAPTER IV: DECADE OF PEACE

¹For a full account of this capable soldier-diplomat, see *DAB*, I, 480-81

²Quoted by Hutton, A. J. W., *Some Historical Material Concerning the History of Chambersburg*, Chambersburg: Franklin Repository, 1930, 2

³*ibid.*

⁴Burgner, M. K., "The Early Travelled Highways about Upper Strasburg," *KHSP*, X, 401-02

⁵*ibid.*, 400

⁶Seilhamer, G. O., "Old Conococheague Families," *KHSP*, II, 294

⁷See Foreman, H. E., "The Forbes Road, Parnell's Knob to Cowan's Gap," *KHSP*, XIII, 309 for an excellent map in two parts, reconstructed by the author

⁸See Orr, J. G., "Early Highways: The Three Mountain Road I," *KHSP*, V, 9; "Fords, Ferries, and Bridges," *KHSP*, IX, 462; and "Sketch of Salem Church, Pleasant Hall, Pennsylvania," *KHSP*, IX, 618

⁹Quoted by Brereton, T. J., "John Wilkins, a Merchant of Carlisle in 1793 — His Ancestry and Autobiography," *KHSP*, III, 217

¹⁰Spessard, H. W., "The Early History of the Falling Spring Presbyterian Church and the Founder of Chambersburg," *KHSP*, XI, 85

¹¹See Heathcote, Rev. C. W., "Lutheran Churches in the Cumberland Valley," *KHSP*, VII, 106

¹²Quoted from *Public Opinion*, Chambersburg, 14 June 1975

¹³Foltz, M. A., "A Backward Glance at the Traits, Traditions and Personality of the Early Scotch-Irish," *KHSP*, IV, 16

¹⁴McKnight, Charles, *Our Western Border One Hundred Years Ago*, Philadelphia: McCurdy, 1879, 200-01

¹⁵Alexander, Professor M. R., "The Schools of Our Fathers," *KHSP*, II, 170-71

¹⁶For this delightful bit of word-play we are indebted to Gordy, U. L., "The Chambersburg Academy," *KHSP*, IX, 557. Thalamos = chamber; polis = city

[17]Orr J. G., "Early Grist Mills of Lurgan Township," *KHSP*, III, 127

[18]McCauley, I. H., *Historical Sketch of Franklin County, Pennsylvania*, Chambersburg: D. F. Pursel, 1877-78, 32

CHAPTER V: THE REVOLUTIONARY YEARS

[1]Clark, D. M., *British Opinion and the American Revolution*, New Haven: Yale University Press, 1930, 126-27. The footnote cites George Heathcote, *A Letter to the Right Honourable the Lord Mayor, the Worshippful Aldermen and Common Council*, London, 1762, p. 10

[2]*ibid.*, 272-73. The quoted portions are taken from *The Present State of the Nation*, 1768 (2nd edition), attributed to William Knox, p. 78

[3]Fiske, John, *The American Revolution*, New York: Houghton, Mifflin & Co., 1896, II, 306-07

[4]Rupp, I. D., *op. cit.*, 403-04

[5]Chambers, *op. cit.*, 93. He quotes the letter from *American Archives*, II, 516

[6]Seilhamer, G. O., "Missing Branches of Our Oldest Family," *KHSP*, IV, 176. Other sources give the date of departure as June, not July. See Chambers, *op. cit.*, 95

[7]McCauley, I. H., *op. cit.*, 74. The author quotes this account from Thatcher's "military journal"

[8]Garrard, L. H., *Chambersburg in the Colony and in the Revolution*, Philadelphia, 1856, 43-4

[9]*ibid.*, 44-45. G. O. Seilhamer states that young Benjamin was born on 4 January 1764. Thus he would be twelve years old. See "Missing Branches of Our Oldest Family," *KHSP*, IV, 181

[10]*History of Franklin County, Pennsylvania,* Chicago: Warner, Beers & Co., 1887, I, 176

[11]Rosters of men from Lurgan, Letterkenny, Montgomery, Peters, and Hamilton townships may be seen in this same volume, pp. 181-84

[12]Chambers, *op. cit.,* 96

[13]McCauley, *op. cit.,* 85

[14]Warner, Rev. R. A., "Reflections Beside the Old Spring at Middle Spring," *KHSP,* XV, 338

[15]*History of Franklin County* (see 10 above), 184

[16]Nevin, Alfred, *Churches of the Valley,* Philadelphia: Wilson, 1852, 185-87

[17]Garrard, *op. cit.,* 49-51

[18]Seilhamer, G. O., *op. cit.,* 177

[19]*ibid.,* 177-78

[20]Garrard, L. H., *op. cit.,* 49-51

[21]*ibid.,* 51-2

[22]*op. cit.,* 178-79

[23]Garrard, L. H., *op. cit.,* 58

[24]Burgner, M. K., "Major James McCalmont," *KHSP,* IX, 382

[25]Orr, J. G., "Early Grist Mills of Lurgan Township," *KHSP,* III, 124. See also Rohr, Sara D., "Margaret Cochran Corbin," *KHSP,* XV, 28; Ross, Emily, "Captain Molly, Forgotten Heroine of the Revolution," in *The Daughters of the American Revolution Magazine,* Feb. 1972, 109; and an editorial in *Public Opinion,* Chambersburg, 15 April 1975

[26]Finafrock, J. L. "The Cumberland County Frontier in the Revolution," *KHSP,* X, 361

[27]Chambers, George, *op. cit.,* 107

[28]Stoner, *op. cit.,* 392

[29]Chambers, *op. cit.,* 109

[30]Fiske, *op. cit.*, 305-06

[31]Quoted by Stonesifer, P. T., "Mad Anthony Wayne," *KHSP*, XII, 305

CHAPTER VI: GROWTH AND CONSOLIDATION

[1]Stoner, J. H., *Historical Papers, Franklin County and the Cumberland Valley, Pennsylvania*, Chambersburg: Craft Press, 1947, 433

[2]Seilhamer, G. O., "Old Conococheague Families," *KHSP*, II, 299

[3]Davison, W. R., "Historical Sketch of East Conococheague Church," *KHSP*, XI, 589

[4]McCauley, *op. cit.*, 113

[5]Churchill, *op. cit.*; McCauley, *op. cit.*, 62

[6]See Maclay, Dr. J. P. "History of the Early Physicians of Chambersburg," *KHSP*, IX, 479 ff.

[7]McCauley, *op. cit.*, 32

[8]*ibid.*, 58

[9]Horst, Mrs. E. H., "Some Interesting Elections in Franklin County," *KHSP*, XV, 79-80

[10]Collins, Rev. E. V., "The Episcopal Church in the Cumberland Valley," *KHSP*, VI, 51

[11]Bambrick, Col. W. C., "Scotland Village," *KSHP*, X, 27; and Kauffman, M. E., "The Covenanter Pew from Corker Hill," *KHSP*, XV, 187

[12]Reiley, Rev. J. McK., "When Methodist Circuit Riders First Came to Franklin County (Pa.)," *KHSP*, XII, 10

[13]Burkholder, Alton, *The Birth of Corpus Christi Parish*, published at the time of the 175th anniversary of the Parish, n. pub., 1967, 6

[14]Gordy, U. L., "Franklin County in the Making of Our Constitution," *KHSP*, XI, 514-16

[15]*American Revolutionary Soldiers of Franklin County, Pennsylvania,* complied by Virginia Shannon Fendrick for the Franklin County Chapter of the Daughters of the American Revolution, Chambersburg, 1969, 162

[16]Diehl, Mary McIlvaine, *Chambersburg and the Chambers Family,* MS of a paper read before the Afternoon Club of Chambersburg, 2 March 1949, 4

[17]McCauley, *op. cit.,* 37-8

[18]*ibid.,* 60

[19]See Hutton, A. J. W., *Some Historical Data Concerning the History of Chambersburg,* Chambersburg: Franklin Repository, 1930, 12-13

[20]McCauley, *op. cit.,* 41

[21]Orr, J. G., "Early Highways IV" *KHSP,* IV, 173, in describing the year 1793, speaks of the Chambers mill as running before 1785 but "torn down a few years since". Thus the Chambers mill must have ceased operation c. 1788-91

[22]Hutton, A. J. W., "Epitaphs and Other Matters of Local Interest," *KHSP,* XIV, 11 says the "only authentic information as to how old he (Benjamin Chambers) was at the time of his death" is the inscription on the grave-stone.

EPILOGUE

[1]See Orr, J. G., "The Whiskey Insurrection," *KHSP,* I, 41

[2]Stoner, J. H., *Historical Papers,* Chambersburg: Craft Press, 1947, 397

[3]Humrich, C. P., "The Relations Which the People of Cumberland and Franklin Counties Bore to the Whisky Insurrection of 1794," *KHSP,* III, 223

[4]Fisher, S. G., *Pennsylvania: Colony and Commonwealth*, Philadelphia: Coates, 1897, 394

[5]Humrich, *op. cit.*, 226

[6]*ibid.*, 227-28

[7]McCauley, *op. cit.*, 48-9

[8]Goodcharles, F. A., *Chronicles of Central Pennsylvania*, III, 105

[9]Orr, J. G., *op. cit.*, 45

[10]Stoner, J. H., *op. cit.*, 402-03

[11]See *KHSP*, XI, 19

[12]Chambers, George, *A Tribute* . . ., Chambersburg: M. A. Foltz, 1871, 165

APPENDIX A

Imaginary Incident: Middle Spring, July 1730

They sat around a smouldering campfire, the four brothers. It was very warm and humid, and the fire was not for comfort: only the remains of the fire on which they had cooked their supper of venison and rice. But it was comforting and permitted them to see one another—the only light they had. Venison from the forest; rice from a bag that Benjamin had carried. They finished off with plums from a tree beside the spring. As for the rice, it was not hard to find it at Harris' Ferry or to buy it from an intinerant trader.

"Are you going to settle here?" asked James, the eldest.

"Yes," said Robert. "I like this place." He looked around thoughtfully and appraisingly. "It has water and wood and grazing land. At least it will have when I clear it a bit."

"What about you, James?" Robert asked. "What do you want to do?"

"Well, I like the land around the Big Spring. It looks fertile and no one has tried to occupy it yet. I think I'll settle there—unless one of you wants it?" He looked at the other two. "No? All right. That's for me!"

"And you, Ben?"

"A few days ago I went prospecting to the southwest. I found a place where a gushing stream pours into a larger stream that the Indians call Conococheague. They said it means 'a long way'. All around it are trees and good ground. It ought to make a good place for a settlement. I think that's where I'll go."

Joseph said quietly, "I'll go with Benjamin."

James sat a moment thinking. "All right," he said at last. "That means three settlements by the four of us, each close to the other. A kind of Chambers sequence. But—" and he looked sharply at Benjamin, "do you think you can make a go of a settlement by those streams? What will you do? How will you make a living? You are only 21. Are you wise to think of doing this?"

James was only a few years older than Benjamin and he had a strong affection for his youngest brother. He thought Benjamin was impulsive, as older brothers often do, and wanted to shield him from any mistakes or danger. Ben sensed this; and, while he acknowledged inwardly his gratitude to James, he could only burst out:

"I can do it! I've seen the place! It's beautiful and perfect for a mill—plenty of water—trees—some open ground—everything. I must go and build a mill and make a place for myself. You will come and see in a year or two! And maybe there will be a settlement there some day. Who knows?"—this with a shrug of the shoulders— "maybe I can make a little colony that will rival yours at Big Spring and Middle Spring!"

He turned and grinned at his brothers in a friendly and affectionate way. For he loved them indeed, and they loved him—had even spoiled him a bit since he was the youngest; and being the youngest, he needed their understanding and support. They were assured and mature; he was not yet fully formed. But of the four he had the genius, the *élan vital*, the imagination to foresee and shape the future. We hear little of the settlements of the older boys. Of Benjamin's settlement there is a notable history.

APPENDIX   B

Imaginary Incident: The Indians Visit Chambers's Mills

Quietly, peacefully, in two and threes, they came to Chambers's mills. They had never seen anything like this and they were fascinated. The grist mill was a big noisy thing, with upper millstone turning relentlessly against the nether, and ground grain appearing like a strange white beard at the side.

Benjamin Chambers liked to have the Indians watch his mill. Their wonder and their approval pleased him. Now and again he would funnel some flour into a small sack—or into an Indian leather pouch—and say with a smile, "Here, take this to your squaw. Tell her to mix it with a little water and a dash of salt and bake it. You will like the bread!" And his Indian friends carried the flour away, did as they were told to do, and of course returned soon for another 'present'.

And the saw mill. Even more than the grist mill it attracted the red men at first. Why? Because it made a great noise. The grist mill was noisy with the sound of the millstones grinding away and the rush of the water over the mill wheel. But this was nothing compared to the loud and strident sound of a circular saw, driven by abundant water power, cutting the length of a bole of a tree. This was indeed a revelation. The whole length of a tree, sawed perfectly from end to end, by a metal object like a plate with teeth on the periphery! When the sawed planks fell away from the saw, the Indians' response was the grunt they always made when they were surprised or pleased. Benjamin watched them from the corner of his eye. He liked to astonish them, and he was always pleased when he did. Normal human response. He smiled to himself.

217

But the saw mill did not excite their envy, only their intense interest. The magic cutting of the long tree-trunks was something for the white man. He needed the planks for his houses; they needed only wigwams. For them the grist mill was the darling object. The white man needed flour; so did they. If there was longing in their hearts, it was for the grist mill. The tragedy is that they later nearly exterminated the grist mills and the owners of them without getting flour for themselves.

APPENDIX   C

I am indebted to Mrs. Lucy Chambers Benchoff for these details. Mrs. Benchoff also states that Col. Chambers and his wife visited Great Britain a third time, leaving two or three children with Col. Chambers's sisters. The purpose again was twofold: to settle his wife's property and to hasten the arrival of Charles Mason and Jeremiah Dixon. In this second errand he was again representing the Penns. As Mason and Dixon arrived in Philadelphia in 1763, this journey must have occurred before that date.

Mrs. Benchoff states further that this trip included a visit to Paris, where husband and wife purchased clothing. Chambers also bought a watch that chimed the hours. Later, when he was in a field outside his fort, some Indians hidden in the bushes heard the chime go off and began shooting at Chambers. He reached safety, but the arrows left marks in the wooden door. These marks may still be seen at 297 Philadelphia Avenue.

Mrs. Benchoff traces the family to the Norman Conquest of 1066, at which time the name was Chambre. The Conqueror gave Chambre land "in the shadow of

Edinburgh". The father of the four Chambers brothers was Major James Chambers, a second son, in the service of William III. He never came to America. The grandfather, another Benjamin Chambers, came to America on the ship *Welcome* with William Penn and during the passage drafted wills for several of the passengers. He remained in America for four or five years before returning home. The family emigrated to Ulster in 1625.

APPENDIX D

Imaginary Incident: Armstrong's Visit to Chambers

Armstrong came to Chambers's mill one day in April of 1748. This was unusual. Armstrong kept to himself near Campbellstown (later St. Thomas). He was solitary and taciturn. But today his face showed he was worried. His cheeks were red and his eyes glittered.

"Chambers, there's trouble coming," he said. "I fear it's bad trouble." He looked down at his moccasins—all the men wore Indian footgear. "Yes, bad trouble!"

Benjamin Chambers hesitated. He liked Armstrong, but he did not think his judgment was always good. They had had some differences of opinion about the Rocky Spring Church. Armstrong thought a new roof was needed, but Chambers was not convinced. Well, that decision could wait. Armstrong was worried now and Benjamin Chambers should hear him out.

"It's the Indians," Armstrong said finally. "The Indians are very nervous. They are engaging in war-dances, painting their faces and breasts for combat, acting very strange and unfriendly. I don't like it. I live a few miles west of you, and I'll catch it before you do." He looked sidewise at Benjamin and paused. "What do you think? What should we do? I said I'd catch it before you do, but you'll catch it, too!"

Chambers hesitated. He too had heard rumors; he too knew the Indians were winding themselves up for something, but his relations with the Indians had always been peaceful, even friendly, throughout the 18 years he had lived beside the Falling Spring.

"Probably they're firing themselves up for an attack on another tribe?" he asked tentatively. He did not really think so, but perhaps he hoped that was the cause of the Indians' warlike posture.

"No, it isn't that," Armstrong replied. "I wish it were. But they burnt an old abandoned log cabin in Path Valley last night. No one there. And they shot a fire arrow over McDowell's mill today. It fell in the Conococheague and there was no damage. But how could you have a clearer warning of trouble to come?"

Benjamin Chambers rose from his chair. He was almost as much impressed by the volubility of this usually silent man as by what he said. Every word, every gesture, every expression bespoke urgency.

"Yes! We must do something at once. If the Indians see us rallying together, they will have second thoughts about burning any more cabins or shooting more fire arrows.

"You rouse the men in the West Conococheague Settlement—all of them. Tell them to meet at McDowell's mill tomorrow noon. I'll ride to the East Conococheague Settlement and spread the word there. Be quick now! We'll meet tomorrow!"

They met, several score of them from a distance of several miles—men also from Lurgan, Letterkenny, Southampton townships and from Path and Horse Valleys. As they gathered beside the mill, they saw smoke rising to the west. A man came running toward them, distraught.

"My cabin's burnt!" he cried, "and my only cow carried off!"

"How about your family?" shouted someone.

"Gone this morning to see friends near Church Hill, thank God!" he replied.

This was how the Associators of the lower Cumberland Valley converted themselves into a provincial militia. They elected Benjamin Chambers colonel; and thereafter the safety of the Conococheague Settlements and the surrounding regions was in their hands. Armstrong had aroused Chambers, and Chambers and he had aroused the three Settlements. The Indians watched and were wary. They did not cause much trouble for several years.

APPENDIX E

Imaginary Incident: Col. Chambers's Swivels

A man who had two swivel guns, four-pounders at that, on the top of his fort was monarch of all he surveyed. No one could dispute him without total danger to life.

This protection gave Col. Chambers great satisfaction. He did not expect trouble from the Indains, for his conduct toward them was kind, courteous, and always peaceful. He understood their ways, talked with them in their language about their needs and problems, and had their respect because they knew he was honest and trustworthy. This was good, he acknowledged. But why not make certain peace doubly certain? Why not give the Indians notice of the strength of the fort?—without any assumption that the Indians would want—or dare—to attack it?

Thus Col. Chambers made a practice of firing at least one of his swivels with a blank charge each week, usually on a Friday, so as to warn the more fractious of the Indians not to become uproarious or destructive over the weekend. The blank charge made a noise that could be heard for a mile or more in all directions.

This firing was a symbol of protection to the inhabitants of Chambers-Town and of power and defense to the Delawares and Shawanese. There was a tradition that, because Friday had so long been the day of firing, the Indians came from the forest and waited on Friday for the explosion, marvelling at its power, at the gunsmoke, and at the white man's ingenuity. Then back to the forests behind the Kittochtinny Mountains.

APPENDIX   F

Imaginary Incident: Shingas

Benjamin Chambers was resting after lunch on a warm October day, dozing in his chair. He had been up early to repair a worn cog in his grist mill and had worked all morning at it. Though he had worked carefully and had changed his clothes before lunch, there were still traces of flour on his shirt. He was tired. It had been this way for a week: mud in the water that fouled the mill race; a bad leak in the roof of the saw mill, wetting the carefully seasoned logs and making them unfit for cutting for three months; a broken arm for Julio, the Indian boy whom he had befriended and trained to feed the logs into the mill. Life was difficult. Always something. Moreover, he had felt a twinge of pain in his right shoulder. "Rheumatism," he thought. He was fifty now. You had to expect such things.

His wife came in, saw him sleeping, and hesitated. She knew how tired he was. She had seen his weary eyes and heard his lowered voice. But she believed she had to wake him. He would know it was important.

"Ben!" she said softly. Then louder, "Ben!" He opened his eyes, turned in his chair, and closed his eyes again.

"Ben! Please listen! You must. Shingas is here. He needs you!"

"Shingas?" he asked wondering. "What's he's doing here?" Shingas was king of the Delawares, deadly foe of the settlers at the Coves and at Fort McCord. His name meant death wherever he went. He was public enemy number one. What was he doing here? Was it a ruse, another treacherous attack on the white man?

"Yes, Shingas," said Jane. "He has no weapons but he has a great swollen jaw. He says he will make a treaty never to attack a white man again if you will take away the pain. He was very polite to me, and I could see that he was suffering. Please come and see him. You might be able to help, and this might end the terror. Think what it would mean if you could make a friend of Shingas!"

Slowly Benjamin Chambers rose. "I'll talk to him, but it goes hard to do it. He was brutal to the people at Cove Gap. He deserves to be scalped, not healed."

And so, grumbling and angry and unsure of himself, Benjamin Chambers went out to Shingas. The Indian chief, inured through long discipline to endure pain, looked nevertheless almost pathetic. He held his hand to his face and bent forward as if in great pain. When Benjamin Chambers came to him, he made a little bow, something Chambers had never seen an Indian do. Then he spoke.

"White man help red man. Red man have hurt in face. See!" When he removed his hand, Benjamin saw indeed. There was a great swelling under the right jaw.

"Let me look!" said Benjamin. He studied the exterior carefully and then—though Shingas winced—drew the lip away from the jaw until the abscess was clearly visible. It looked nasty. Benjamin knew it would be very painful to open it and sterilize it. How much could Shingas stand before he lost control and throttled Benjamin? He was large and powerful and could easily do it.

Benjamin looked at Shingas thoughtfully and waited. Shingas said, "Help me, white man. Pain hurt!"

"But I make you more pain to cure you. You brave? You no mind hurt?"

Shingas's lip quivered because he did not know, despite rigid Indian discipline and self-control, whether he could stand much more. Benjamin Chambers saw the quiver, respected it as an indication of the great suffering Shingas felt, and turned toward his tooth-chest to find his lancet and his floss.

"I let you give me more pain!"

This was all Benjamin needed to know. King Shingas was in extremity. The tooth was more important than everything, even than his campaign against the white man. Not exactly the tooth, but relief from the exquisite hurting.

Benjamin was, as we well know, not a dentist, but in his frontier life he had had to be all things to all men; and among his many skills was what the frontier men called 'tooth-pulling'. Really it was more than that. Benjamin had learned from medical books he had brought from England, carefully selected to be useful on his Pennsylvania frontier, that an oral abscess could easily be relieved if one were careful to avoid infection. He also knew there would be danger of septicemia; and if Shingas were to die, what would his warriors' revenge be? Benjamin quailed at the thought.

But he was well aware that, if he could help Shingas, great benefits might come to the white man. He decided to take the risk and prepared his treatment·very carefully. It was one of the great moments of his life. Abscess, pain, war? Or relief, gratitude, peace?

Everything turned on the lancet and the floss—and on King Shinga's endurance. Benjamin held his lancet up so that Shingas could see it.

"This will draw off the abscess," he said. "Must make tiny hole in side to let out evil spirit. This hurt but not more than ache you feel now. Then I press gently on side—" Benjamin made the motion but did not touch the jaw, "and catch evil spirit in floss." —which he held up. He knew the Indian mind. Surprise an Indian, and you get an instinctive violent response. Show him beforehand, and he may control himself. *May.* There was always a risk that he would or could not. This was the risk Benjamin had resolved to take.

The critical moment had come. He made Shingas sit down on a log. Then gently he pulled the lip downward, revealing the ugly white head of the swelling. Shingas trembled but did not move. With a quick thrust learned from other lancings, Benjamin pushed the lancet home, just deep enough but not too deep. When he withdrew it, he caught the 'evil spirit' on the floss very skillfully.

"Do not swallow!" cried Benjamin in a sharp voice. "Sit very still. It is going well. Already some of the pain has gone!"

Benjamin Chambers could see beads of sweat on Shingas's face. He understood how well the chief was behaving. Could he risk the next and necessary step? Could he press the abscess and empty it? Would Shingas be equal to that?

Benjamin knew, of course, that he must try.

"Now I hurt you more, but not much more. Must get all evil spirit out. Must press hurting place. You be brave. Then you get well!"

Shingas was brave. Benjamin washed the wound, made Shingas flush his mouth several times, and treated the wound with a poultice of tobacco and thyme. He covered it with a bandage and instructed Shingas not to remove the bandage and to return in 48 hours.

So was King Shingas cured of his pain. Later Benjamin had to pull the offending tooth and open the abscess a second time; but this was nothing compared to the first treatment.

"Well," said Benjamin a month later to Jane, "I'm glad that incident's over. Shingas sweated through it, but I sweated more. I never knew when he might swing his great fist and smash my face, but he didn't, and that was all I asked."

"Maybe you made a friend of him for life. You know how the Indians are; do them a favor and they'll never harm you."

Shingas never attacked a white man again, and later he and Benjamin Chambers were linked as blood brothers in a solemn Indian rite.

APPENDIX   G

A Wise Old Indian Speaks of Matrimony

Extant records bear occasional comments by Indians on the ways of the white man. Here is one:

An aged Indian, who, for many years, had spent much time among the white people, both in Pennsylvania and New Jersey, one day, about the year 1770, observed that the Indians had not only a much easier way of getting a wife than the whites, but also a more certain way of getting a good one. "For", said he, in broken English, "White man court—court—may be one whole year! May be two years before he marry! Well, may be then he get very good wife—but may be not—may be very cross! Well, now, suppose cross! scold so soon as get awake in morning! scold all day! scold until sleep!—all one—he must keep him—white people have law forbidding throw away wife if he be ever so cross—must keep him always! Well, how does Indian do? Indian, when he see industrious squaw, he go to him, place his two forefingers close aside each other, make two like one—then look squaw in the face—see him smile—this is all—he say, yes!—so he take him home—no danger he be cross! No, no—squaw know too well what Indian do if he cross! throw him away and take another! Squaw love to eat meat—no husband no meat. Squaw do everything to please husband, he do everything to please squaw—live happy."

—McKnight, Charles, Our Western Border, 751.

The character of George III will probably remain an enigma to all successive generations. Fiske (as we have just seen) calls him a "half crazy young king", but he was not truly mad until late in life. The contemporary biographer John Wain writes of him:

> In contrast with his two previous namesakes, George was a constitutional monarch; he ruled very much with the consent of Parliament, determinedly hostile to the King and the 'King's friends' who in 1780 tabled [*i.e.*, proposed] the celebrated motion that 'the influence of the monarchy has increased, is increasing, and ought to be diminished'. Johnson might well have felt that to undermine the power of the King was merely to put more power into the hands of the rich and aristocratic Whigs, who were no more democratic than the King and far less accountable to public criticism.[1]

This reading of his character makes him less an autocratic and authoritarian monarch than do Fiske and others in this country, and it implies that his actions in general had the sanction of Parliament. Thus he did not, as so many have said, act solely on his own.

Samuel Johnson—the celebrated Dr. Johnson, regent of English letters in the mid-eighteenth century—had an interview with the King at Buckingham House, site of the present Buckingham Palace, in 1767. Boswell's account of it, brought to us by Wain, sheds further light on the sovereign:

[1]Wain, John, *Samuel Johnson, A Biography*. New York: Viking Press, 1974, 299
[2]*Ibid.*

The interview seems to have pleased both men. Johnson, though his attitude was one of profound respect, made no attempt to speak in the hushed undertone that people usually adopt on these occasions; his voice was 'resonant' (Boswell's word); he evidently showed his habitual blend of respect for hierarchy and degree with self-esteem. The King, for his part, took the trouble to pay Johnson a compliment. On Johnson's remarking of himself that he 'thought he had already done his part as a writer', George replied, 'I should have thought so too, if you had not written so well.' This, Johnson remarked afterward, was a compliment 'fit for a King to pay. It was decisive!' Asked whether he had made any reply, he said firmly. 'No, Sir. When the King had said it, it was to be so. It was not for me to bandy civilities with my Sovereign.[2]

However hateful and egocentric a character he has been made out to be by some historians, this vignette shows him to have been both gentle and tactful. There is no reason to believe that the report of this incident is colored by bias. The words are verbatim, sincere, and honorable.

The reservations offered here do not vitiate Fiske's conclusions about the heinous Coercion Acts, but they may cast light upon the character of the King.

APPENDIX   I

Imaginary Incident: Captain James Goes to War

It was late afternoon in the last week of April, 1775. James was tired. There had been some trouble with the grist mill—mud or pebbles in the water wheel. He had had to get quite wet before the trouble was cured. And also one of the cows had strayed away—one of the best milch cows—and no one had been able to find her. Worries. Always problems. One of his worries was his father, who had had more attacks of rheumatism lately.

But he was not downhearted. It was almost supper time and he could smell the scent of venison, potatoes, and that most delicious Epicurean morsel, new peas, coming from the kitchen. He sighed with contentment, closed his eyes, and rested from a day of weary work.

There was a determined knock on the door. "What's that?" he said vacantly, still half asleep. Into the room without ceremony burst Pompey, the family servant. Pompey was gregarious and always knew what was going on.

"Sir!" he cried, "have ye heard the news? The British and the Americans had a battle on the 19th at Concord. Many killed, both sides!"

"What's all this, Pompey?" James replied, rubbing his eyes. "Calm yourself and tell me what happened. Sit down and catch you breath. If you don't, you'll be speechless in two minutes!" James's tone implied he was a bit annoyed by Pompey's uninvited arrival.

Pompey sat on a chest in the corner, not wishing to intrude into a chair. James watched him closely, seeing that he was greatly excited and flushed in the face.

"A courier just came from Carlisle. He say battle in Massachusetts. All New England angry, in arms. British shoot Minutemen at Concord, but Minutemen kill many British on retreat toward Boston. They're calling for men in Carlisle. Bad. Bad!"

Captain James listened carefully. The news was not

altogether unexpected. Other couriers had told of the Tea Party, of British reinforcements in Boston, of American troops watching from the surrounding hills. It was a situation, he thought, that was bound to explode. And now the explosion had come.

Catherine entered the room and stopped suddenly when she saw James and Pompey. "Why are they so grim?" she thought. "Has something happened?"

"It's supper time," she said, pretending that nothing was different from last evening. "Come—you too, Pompey—we have fresh venison and some peas from the new garden—very early this year!"

James turned slowly in his chair.

"Yes," he said thoughtfully. "But then I must go at once to Carlisle. Things have happened this week. I must talk with Col. Armstrong."

He paused and then turned to face her. "Kitty, I may have to leave you and the children and the mill. It looks like a war. Blood's been spilt at Concord in Massachusetts, and there's a call for men to resist the redcoats and protect Boston. Heaven knows where it will all lead, but I may have to go and fight!"

Catherine shrank against the door, forgetting her kitchen for the moment.

"Oh, no, James! You can't leave us alone! What will the Indians do to us if we are alone here? We'll all be killed like Enoch's pupils ten years ago!"

"No," he replied quietly. "No. The Indians won't give any trouble now. You'll have the boys to protect you and the neighbors. But I don't know what my duty is. I must see Armstrong and find out. We've got to stand up for our rights, that's sure! I haven't got anything against the British—after all we were born British subjects—but

231

King Geroge and Lord North have trampled the rights of American British subjects and we've got to do something now!"

Armstrong and James's father had had some fiery words about Benjamin's cannons 20 years ago, but that was forgotten now. Armstrong didn't hold grudges. He said, "Chambers, are you willing to lead a battalion of local men? We need arms as well as men, but I think you can get both!"

Soon the men were assembled, armed, and eager to march. They wasted no time. First to Harris' Ferry, then across country to Reading, across Connecticut and thus to Boston. They marched both fast and in good order. The people whom they passed *en route* cheered them and admired their military bearing. They wore their doeskin fringed jackets and round hats, a novelty to all who saw them pass. And every man carried his long-barrelled rifle.

They arrived in Boston on 7 August, the first troops from the hinterland. Everyone wondered at them. Conservative and conventional New Englanders had never seen men like this, most of them six feet tall or more, from the distant frontier of which they had only heard or read.

"From southern Pennsylvania? Where's that? . . But aren't they handsome! They look as if they could give the British stroke for stroke! See that man with the extra-long rifle? . . And the captain—isn't he almost regal in his bearing? . . Have they all horses like these in Pennsylvania? . . They say the boy is the captain's son. He's certainly a good-looking lad! Poor boy, though . . .

He's too young to go off to war, even with his father to look after him. I hope he'll be all right!"

Salute. Col. Armstrong bowed to the Commander-in-Chief. "Reporting for duty, General. The First Pennsylvania Line after a rapid march!"

"Greetings to you, Colonel, and to you, Captain! You are the first to arrive in response to the call of Congress. We are grateful, and the Continental Army is much strengthened by your presence. More, I am sure, will follow your example and we shall soon have an army capable of meeting our foes on even terms."

Later General Washington invited James to dinner. There was the usual military chatter and gossip, but finally Washington turned to James.

"Your men are sharpshooters? That is their reputation. Do they shoot well?"

"Very well," replied James quickly. "They grew up on the Pennsylvania frontier, as you know. Before they were fifteen years old they could shoot a squirrel at 50 yards. At 20 they could shoot an Indian at 150 yards. You can trust them. They can even shoot a target moving in the air, like a wild turkey—and that with a rifle!"

Washington was silent for some time, thinking, wondering about tomorrow and food for the army and medical supplies in case he had to attack. Then he turned toward James and said in a low but earnest voice, "We shall expect good things of your men from the Pennsylvania frontier who can shoot Indians at 150 yards. Often we shall meet our enemies at fewer yards than that. Tell them never to waste ammunition and always to shoot true to the mark!"

James nodded; and seeing that the General was

233

preoccupied with plans for tomorrow, he thanked his host and returned, somehow uplifted in spirit, to his quarters. He had been in the presence of a great man. The memory of this conversation carried him through many difficult days ahead.

APPENDIX J

Imaginary Incident: Young Ben at Brandywine

Col. James and his men were straining to heave the heavy artillery piece away from the now broken battle line. Its very size and power had given the American troops great hopes, but now its weight was only a liability. The word had come to abandon it, but Col. James knew how valuable it would be to future campaigns and was determined to save it. Bullets were spattering all around, but they had moved the cannon a hundred yards and believed they could save it.

Suddenly a bullet struck Col. James in the side. He cried out and fell; but soon he was on his feet again.

Gasping, he shouted, "It's nothing! Come on! Get this piece over the hill where the cavalry can protect it!"

As they topped the hill and the enemy's fire fell short, James looked up and saw Ben sitting beneath a tree. He looked white and there was pain written on his face. He had stripped off his trousers, and from his right thigh blood oozed and ran down his leg. Col. James's heart nearly stopped.

"Ben! What is it?" he cried, forgetting his own pain and dropping on his knees beside the boy. The rest of the men saw this, and a sergeant called out, "You look after him, sir. He's a good man. We'll get the cannon away!"

"He's a good man," thought James. "Yes, but only a boy still. God grant he'll be all right!"

The surgeon said it was a piece of shapnel about two inches long. Not too much blood had been lost, but the metal had to be removed at once to prevent infection.

"Can he stand some pain?" asked the medical men.

"I think so," replied James, looking uneasily at Ben's white face and pain-drawn lips.

There were no anaesthetics then. An operation of this sort was very painful and many men fainted and some died. Col. James held his breath and his brow was moist as the surgeon cut away Ben's flesh and probed and finally brought out a piece of metal. Ben was pale and cold and his teeth gritted together, but he never uttered a sound. Col. James held the boy's hand throughout the operation, and more than anything else Ben's grip told his father what the suffering was and also what self-control the boy had. The surgeon dressed the wound and Ben sighed deeply, smiled at his father, and within a few minutes was asleep.

"He'll be all right," the surgeon said. "He's young and in fine health. But what about you, sir?" James had almost forgotten the wound in his side.

"Look at it, will you?" he asked.

"It's a bullet, I think, in the soft flesh", he said as his fingers probed gently. "No danger of a damaged organ, but we'll have to get it out or there will be infection, even gangrene. Shall we go after it now, sir?"

James thought a moment.

"No", he said finally, "unless you say a few days' delay will be dangerous. I've had about all I can take today—the battle and Ben's wound and this. Can I wait?"

"Certainly you can," replied the surgeon. "A few days anyway. But don't wait too long. You never know what these lead bullets will do to human flesh!"

Before he turned in that night, exhausted though he was physically and emotionally, Col. James wrote a brief letter and sent it to the adjutant with instructions to have it delivered as soon as possible.

Dearest Kitty,

We are all right, Ben and I. Don't worry.

Ben caught a bit of British shell in his right thigh. The surgeon cut it out and Ben is asleep now. I have a bullet in my left side in a harmless place. We'll cut it out later. Not much pain.

Tell Pompey to look carefully after this year's calves and bring in lots of firewood. It'll be a cold winter, they say.

Trust me to look after Ben.

J.C.

Young Ben recovered better than his father. The wound healed, and all that remained was a scar and a slight depression in the thigh. But Col. James, though the bullet was successfully removed, felt pain in his side at certain times throughout the rest of his years.

"Slight price," he ruminated later, "for all we gained in the war. What's a little pain in my side if Ben's all right and taking on the headship of the family?"

APPENDIX K

Alexander Hamilton states the difficulty in *The Federalist or The New Constitution,* No. 15 (1787):

> Those who have been conversant in the proceedings of popular assemblies; who have seen how difficult it often is, where there is no exterior pressure of circumstances, to bring them to harmonious resolutions on important points, will readily conceive how impossible it must be to induce a number of such assemblies, deliberating at a distance from each other, at different times, and under different impressions, long to cooperate in the same views and pursuits . . . Each State yielding to the persuasive voice of immediate interest or convenience, has successively withdrawn its support, till the frail and tottering edifice seems ready to fall upon our heads, and to crush us beneath its ruins.

James Madison, in No. 37 (1788), finds the new Constitution a document that excites admiration and wonder:

> Would it be wonderful if, under the pressure of all these difficulties, the convention should have been forced into some deviations from that artificial structure and regular symmetry which an abstract view of the subject might lead an ingenious theorist to bestow on a Constitution planned in his closet or in his imagination? The real wonder is that so many difficulties should have been surmounted, and surmounted with a unanimity almost as unprecedented as it must have been unexpected. It is impossible for any man of candor to reflect on this circumstance

without partaking of the astonishment. It is impossible for the man of pious reflection not to perceive in it a finger of that Almighty hand which has been so frequently and signally extended to our relief in the critical stages of the revolution.

APPENDIX   L

Imaginary Incident: Capt. James Enlarges Chambersburg

"Kitty," said James after supper on a night in June of 1783, "you know I've bought a large tract of land from the Colonel, my father."

"Yes, I do," Kitty replied. "I don't know what you're going to do with it . . or how you'll pay for it without ruining us!"

James laughed and slapped his knee.

"Pay for it?" he replied. "That's easy. We've had four good years with the farms and the livestock, and I've enough money to pay my father with a good bit left over. Anyway, you know he'd never push me for payment. He said yesterday he thought my idea of expanding his town was excellent. He'd back me to the limit. But I don't need it. I've payed him cash, and it's all settled!"

"Well, that's good," she said somewhat uncertainly. "If we can make a go of it, I think the town will benefit. But are you sure you can finance it?"

She looked at him apprehensively, for—though he had proved a warrior of whom all were proud—he had not had much experience in domestic affairs. He had gone off to join General Washington when other young men of his age were learning the lessons of commerce and trade. He had indeed learned the lessons of war; but as she thought of the other young men his contemporaries, she was dubious about his knowledge of real estate and finance. It was not that she did not trust him. She would always trust him. It was only that she was unsure of his ability in a world other than that of warfare.

"Don't be silly," he replied, filling the pipe Shingas had given his father ten years ago. His father had given it to him as a special token of his affection and respect when he returned from service two years before.

"Don't be silly. I've planned everything. The street that bounds my purchase on the north will be named Catherine Street, for you. To the south we'll lay out lots, as my father did in 1764; and we'll call the new section Chambers Town so as not to confuse it with Chambersburg. You'll see! It'll all go well. We'll have a new portion of our town, and you and I'll make a few dollars in doing so!"

James made a few dollars, but not many, for his native town was growing only slowing in those years. Perhaps the greatest joy he had from this venture was Kitty's pleasure in having a street named for her. She blushed and looked down and then looked up and smiled when he told her of his intention. Later when they had visitors at their house, she almost always took them the few hundred yards to show them Catherine Street. It was muddy and uneven most of the time—especially in the spring when the snows were melting—but James had erected a handsome sign in clear black letters against a white background.

CATHERINE STREET

When she returned home with her friends, her cup was running over.

APPENDIX M

Dinner with President and Mrs. Washington
(Presumably in Philadelphia)

S. R. Diehl, in his article entitled "An Old Home in Path Valley" (*KHSP*, XIV, 131-2), quotes as follows from Maclay's journal:

"The company were President and Mrs. Washington, Vice-President and Mrs. Adams, Mr. Gay and wife, Mr. Langdon and wife, Mr. Dalton and a lady, perhaps his wife, and Mr. Smith, Bassett and myself, Lear and Lewis, the President's two secretaries.

"The President and Mrs. Washington sat opposite each other in the middle of the table. The two secretaries, one at each end. It was a great dinner and the best of the kind ever I was at. The room, however, was disagreeably warm. First was soup; fish, roasted and boiled, meats—gammon, fowls, etc. The middle of the table was garnished in the usual tasty way, with small images, flowers (artificial), etc. The dessert was first apple pies, puddings, etc., then iced creams, jellies, etc., then watermelons, mush-melons, apples, peaches and nuts.

"It was the most solemn dinner I ever sat at. Not a health drank—scarce a word said, until the cloth was taken away. Then the President, taking a glass of wine with great formality, drank to the health of every individual by name round the table. Everybody imitated him, charged glasses; and such a buzz of health, sir, and health, madam, and thank you, sir, and thank you madam, never had I heard before. Indeed I had like to have been thrown out in the harry; but I got a little wine in my glass, and passed the ceremony.

"The ladies sat a good while, and the bottles passed about—but there was a dead silence almost. Mrs. Washington at last withdrew with the ladies. I expected the men would now begin, but the same stillness remained. The President told of a New England clergyman, who had lost a hat and wig in passing a river called Brunks. He smiled and everybody else laughed. The President kept a fork in his hand when the cloth was taken away, I thought for the purpose of picking nuts. He ate no nuts, but played with the fork, striking on the edge of the table with it. We did not sit long after the ladies retired. The President arose and went upstairs to drink coffee. The company followed. I took my hat and came home." We are not to conclude from this recital that Senator Maclay underestimated the first President for in another section of the same diary, he speaks of General Washington as "the greatest man in the world."

APPENDIX   N

FOR COL. BENJAMIN CHAMBERS

You of the mills and the pointed tall stockade,
You who settled beside the Conococheague
Where the Falling Spring together makes a
    league:
You who our frontier habitation made:
You who awaited the deadly Indian raid
And often watched long hours with gun at
    hand,
Fearing the coming of a silent Indian band
Bent on murder and rapine, not on trade:
You of the strong-walled fort and the ready
    gun,

You of the rose-rent that all descendants bring,
You had a deep-held faith in this rugged land.
In your autumn years did you sit by the Falling
   Spring
And, musing, see in that watery mirror-strand
The town that was yet to be, now just begun?

CHRONOLOGICAL TABLE

1558-1603: Queen Elizabeth I

1588: Defeat of Spanish Armada

1597: Ruin of Second Armada

1603: Mountjoy's conquest of Ireland
Accession of James I

1606 onward: Scots to northern Ireland

1625: Accession of Charles I

1641: Massacre in Ireland, October

1642: Puritans in control; theatres closed; civil war
begins

1645: Cromwell's New Model Army

1649: Execution of Charles I, 30 January
Commonwealth proclaimed

1650 ff.: Rise of Cromwell

1653: Oliver Cromwell, Lord Protector

1658: Death of Cromwell, 3 September

1658-60: Richard Cromwell, Lord Protector

1660: The Restoration: Accession of Charles II

1681: Charles II's grant of land to William Penn

1683: Penn arrives in America aboard the ship *Welcome*
Germans settle at Germantown

1685: Accession of James II
Revocation of Edict of Nantes, persecution and
flight of Protestants

1688: The Bloodless Revolution; Bill of Rights

1689: Accession of William III and Mary

1702: Accession of Queen Anne
Second wave of German immigrants from Palatinate begins

c. 1709: Birth of Benjamin Chambers

1713: Tuscaroras defeated by whites in Carolinas; fled north and joined Five Nations

1714: Accession of George I (House of Hanover)

1715: "The Fifteener"

1718-19: Scotch -Irish immigration to America begins

c. 1720: Jacques Letort near Carlisle

c. 1725: Four Chambers brothers arrive in America and settle at Fishing Creek

1727: Accession of George II

1729: Lancaster County established from Chester County

1730: Chambers brothers enter the Great Valley and settle

1732: Temporary Line between Pennsylvania and Maryland

1734: Founding of congregation of Presbyterian Church of the Falling Spring

1736: Treaty with Indians

1737: Walking Purchase

1738: Rocky Spring congregation founded

1741: Hopewell township divided; Hopewell - east; Antrim - west

1742: Benjamin Chambers marries Sarah Patterson

1743: Birth of James Chambers; death of Sarah Patterson Chambers

1744: Great Road built from Harris's Ferry to Williamsport

1746: Battle of Culloden; end of Stuart plot to regain British throne
1748: Militia formed in Cumberland Valley; Benjamin Chambers made colonel

Benjamin Chambers marries Jane Williams
1749: York County established from Lancaster County
1750: Cumberland County established from York County

Burnt Cabins
1754: Indian treaty at Albany

Seven Years' War begins
1755: Braddock's defeat, 9 July

Braddock-Forbes road begun

Indian Terror begins
1756: Forts built in Cumberland Valley

Attack on Kittanning

Lord Loudoun made commander-in-chief of British forces in North America
1758: General Forbes captures Fort Duquesne from French

Pitt recalls Lord Loudoun
1759: Wolfe defeats Montcalm on Heights of Abraham at Quebec, September
1760: Accession of George III

Amherst captures Montreal, 8 September; French Canada now British
1761: Fannett township created

Letterkenny township created from Lurgan township
1763: Treaty of Paris; end of Seven Years' War

Act of Pennsylvania Assembly forbidding sale of arms and powder to Indians

Mason and Dixon begin surveying Pennsylvania - Maryland border, 19 December

1763-64: Pontiac's War.
      Col. Bouquet's campaign
      Paxton Boys
1764: Col. Chambers lays out Chambersburg
      Enoch Brown massacre, 26 July
      Stamp Act Congress, October 5
1765: Stamp Act
      Incident at Fort Loudon
1766: Repeal of Stamp Act
1767: Completion of Mason-Dixon line to point approximately south of Bedford
      New taxes on imports to America
      Boycott of goods from Britain
      John Dickinson's *Letters from a Farmer*
1770: Lord North becomes first minister
      Boston massacre, March
      Founding of First Evangelical Lutheran Church
1771: Francis Asbury comes to America
1772: Committees of Correspondence established in Massachusetts
1773: Boston Tea Party, December
1774: Regulating Act, April; military occupation of Boston; port closed
      Paul Revere visits Philadelphia to solicit aid, 19 May
      Congress assembles at Philadelphia, September
      Freemen of Cumberland County send resolution to Congress
      Col. Chambers conveys to Franklin County land for court house, 28 September
1775: Skirmish at Lexington, 19 April
      Washington made commander-in-chief by Congress, 15 June
      Breed's Hill and Bunker Hill, 17 June

Congress in session at Carpenter's Hall in
Philadelphia
James Chambers and others from the Cumberland
Valley march to Boston; arrive 7 August
Benedict Arnold invades Canada
Ethan Allen and Arnold seize Hudson Valley forts
Tom Paine's *Common Sense*

1776: Declaration of Independence, 2 July
Abolition of Pennsylvania Assembly
New Constitution for Pennsylvania adopted
Battle of Trenton, 25 December
Hessians hired by British to serve in America

1777: Battle of Princeton, 1 January
Tories persecuted in Philadelphia
Battle of Brandywine, 11 September
Capture of Philadelphia by General Howe, 26
September
Surrender of Burgoyne at Saratoga, 17 October
Washington passes winter at Valley Forge

1778: Alliance of France and the United States, 6
January
Howe resigns as commander of British forces;
Clinton succeeds him
Battle of Monmouth Court House, June
Wyoming massacre, 3 July

1779: Declaration of treason and forfeiture of property
John Paul Jones's pyrrhic victory off Flamborough
Head

1780: Founding of Zion Reformed Church
First grammar school in Chambersburg

1781: Col. James Chambers retires from military service,
17 January
Surrender of Cornwallis at Yorktown, 19 October

Law requiring acceptance of depreciated paper money at face value

1782: Lord North resigns

Ministries of Rockinham and Shelburne

Peace negotiations begun

Greencastle laid out

1783: Treaty of Paris, 30 November; formal end of Revolutionary War

First iron works in Valley opened at Mount Pleasant

Town of Concord established

Southampton township formed from Lurgan township

Effects of Industrial Revolution felt in Britain

1784: Franklin County established

First elections in Franklin County held, 12 October

Methodist Church in America organized, 25 December

1787: Constitutional Convention meets in Philadelphia, 24 May

Pennsylvania Legislature meets concurrently with Convention

1788: Death of Col. Benjamin Chambers

Greene Township formed from Letterkenny township

1789: First meeting of House of Representatives and Senate of United States

Bill of Rights; *i.e.*, first ten amendments to Constitution

Washington inaugurated as first President, 30 April

Estates General convened in Paris, 5 May

1791: Congress passes excise law taxing whiskey
1792: Western Pennsylvania counties forward to Congress resolution opposing excise tax, 22 August
1794: State and Federal commissions sent to reason with dissidents, August and September
"Liberty Poles" in Cumberland Valley, September
Military expedition to western Pennsylvania, October
Washington in Chambersburg, October
End of Whiskey Rebellion, November
Franklin County court house built
1795: Death of Jane Williams Chambers
1797: Waynesboro laid out by John Wallace, 29 December
Founding of Chambersburg Academy

BIBLIOGRAPHY

Bietsch, Philip, *Backward Glances,* Chambersburg, 1944

Biographical Annals of Franklin County, Pennsylvania, containing genealogical accounts of representative families, 1905

Burkholder, Alton. *The Birth of Corpus Christi Parish,* published at the time of the 175th anniversary of the Parish. n. pub., 1967

Camp, D. I. and Kaufman, J. W., *History of the Presbyterian Churches of Path Valley,* Chambersburg: Chambersburg Repository, 1916

Chambers, George, *A Tribute to the Principles, Virtues, Habits and Public Usefulness of the Irish and Scotch Early Settlers of Pennsylvania,* Chambersburg: M. A. Foltz, 1871

Churchill, Sir Winston, *The Age of Revolution*, New York: Dodd, Mead Co., 1957

Clark, D. M. *British Opinion of the American Revolution*, Yale University Press, 1930

——————, *The Rise of the British Treasury: Colonial Administration in the Eighteenth Century*, Yale University Press, 1960

Conrad, W., *Conococheague: A History of the Greencastle-Antrim Community, 1736-1971*, Greencastle: Greencastle- Antrim School District, 1971

Dictionary of American Biography, ed. Allen Johnson, New York: Charles Scribner's Sons, 1927 -

Dictionary of National Biography, ed. Sir Leslie Stephen and Sir Sidney Lee, Oxford University Press, 1917 -

Diehl, Mary McIlvaine, *Chambersburg and the Chambers Family*, typed MS of paper read before the Afternoon Club of Chambersburg, 2 March 1949

Donehoo, G. P., *A History of the Cumberland Valley In Pennsylvania*, Harrisburg: The Susquehanna Historical Association, 1930. 2 vv.

Encyclopedia Britannica, New York: Encyclopedia Britannica Company, 11th edition, 1910

The Federalist or The New Constitution, New York, Heritage Press, 1945

Fendrick, V. S. ed., *Revolutionary Soldiers of Franklin County, Pennsylvania*, Chambersburg: Franklin County Chapter of the Daughters of the American Revolution, c. 1944.

Fisher, S. G., *The Making of Pennsylvania*, Philadelphia: J. B. Lippincott, 1896, 1924, 1932

——————, *Pennsylvania: Colony and Commonwealth*, Philadelphia: H. T. Coates Co., 1897

249

Fiske, John, *The American Revolution*, New York: Houghton, Mifflin and Company, 1891, 2 vv.

Foltz, M. A. and Harbaugh, Linn, *Historical Sketch of Zion Reformed Church, 1780-1911*, Chambersburg: Public Opinion Press, 1911

Foreman, Harry E., *The Harry Foreman Collection, 1950-71*, 7 vv.

The Frontier Forts of Pennsylvania, Report of the Commission to Locate the Site of, Harrisburg: William Stanley Ray, State Printer, 2nd edition, Thomas Lynch Montgomery, Litt. D., ed., 1916, 2 vv.

Garrard, L. H., *Chambersburg in the Colony and the Revolution*, Philadelphia, 1856

Green, J. R., *Short History of the English People*, New York: A. L. Burt & Co., c. 1897

Heritage of the Falling Spring, n. pub., n. d.

History of Franklin County, Pennsylvania, Chicago: Warner, Beers & Co., 1887

Hutton, A. J. W., *Some Historical Data Concerning the History of Chambersburg*, Chambersburg: Franklin Repository Press, 1930

Incidents of Border Life, Chambersburg: Pritts, 1839

Kittochtinny Historical Society: 15 vv. of papers read before the Society, 1898 - 1972

McCauley, I. H., *Historical Sketch of Franklin County*, Harrisburg: Patriot Press, 1887-88

McKnight, Charles, *Our Western Border One Hundred Years Ago*, Philadelphia: McCurdy, 1879

Mitchison, Rosalind, *A History of Scotland*, London: Methuen & Co., 1970

Mudge, W. L., *Rocky Spring Presbyterian Church and the Revolutionary Period*, Chambersburg: Franklin County Chapter of the Daughters of the American Revolution, 1919

Nevin, Alfred, *Churches of the Valley*, Philadelphia: Wilson, 1852

Nill, Sidney, *Our Conococheague Settlement, 1732 - 1782*, Chambersburg: Franklin County Chapter of the Daughters of the American Revolution, 1971

Notestein, Wallace, *The Scot in History*, New Haven: Yale University Press, 1946

Pennsylvania Archives, passim.

Rocky Spring Churchyard, published by the Franklin County Chapter of the Daughters of the American Revolution, n.d.

Rupp, I. D., *History and Topography of Dauphin, Cumberland, Franklin, Bedford, Adams, and Perry Counties*, Lancaster City, Pa.: G. Hills, 1846

Schneck, H. P., ed., *History of the Falling Spring Presbyterian Church*, 1894

The Scotch-Irish in America, addresses at the 10th congress in Chambersburg, 3 May - 2 June, 1901, Nashville, Tennessee: Bigham and Smith, c. 1902

Seilhamer, G. O., *Biographical Annals of Franklin County*, Chicago: Genealogical Publishing Co., 1905

Shoemaker, Mrs. Mary W., *Five Typical Scotch-Irish Families of the Cumberland Valley*, Albany, N.Y., 1922

Stewart, Mrs. Harriet Wylie, *History of the Cumberland Valley, Pennsylvania*, n. pub., n.d. (c. 1917)

Stoner, J. H., *Historical Papers, Franklin County and the Cumberland Valley, Pennsylvania*, Chambersburg: Craft Press, 1947

Thayer, Theodore, *Pennsylvania Politics and the Growth of Democracy, 1740 - 76*, publication of the Pennsylvania Historical Commission, Harrisburg, 1963

251

The United Presbyterian Churches of Path and Amberson Valleys, 1766 - 1966, Shippensburg: Beidel Printing House, 1966

Webster, Eleanor M., "Insurrection at Fort Loudon: Rebellion or Preservation of Peace?", *Western Pennsylvania Historical Magazine,* Vol. 47, No. 2, April 1964

INDEX

254